"A survival manual for partners of sex addicts, with step-by-step instructions on coping with betrayal, trauma, and how to set boundaries. Vicki's 5-Step format teaches partners to set boundaries that are empowering, and promote self-care and self-love. This book will be essential reading for recovering partners. I highly recommend it."

Stefanie Carnes, PhD, LMFT
Author of *Mending a Shattered Heart: A Guide for Partners of Sex Addicts* and *Facing Addiction: Starting Recovery from Alcohol and Drugs*

"Vicki Tidwell Palmer guides the reader through a practical and thorough journey to healing. Encouraging partners to move from an exclusive focus on the trauma of infidelity to the possibility of forgiveness, *Moving Beyond Betrayal* is a welcome and much-needed contribution to the self-help literature for the rapidly growing ranks of partners of sex addicts."

Kenneth M. Adams, PhD, CSAT-S
Psychologist and author of *Silently Seduced* and *When He's Married to Mom*

"*Moving Beyond Betrayal* eloquently offers partners a necessary distinction between powerlessness and finding the power to act. A much-needed ingredient for reclaiming the lost 'self' post-betrayal. Vicki's words guide a wounded heart back to respite and healing."

Kelly McDaniel, LPC, NCC, CSAT
Author of *Making Advances: A Comprehensive Guide for Treating Female Sex and Love Addicts* and *Ready to Heal: Breaking Free of Addictive Relationships*

D0250434

"An important resource for wounded partners
who are trying to find their way out of the maze
of trauma caused by their partner's sex addiction.
Vicki Tidwell Palmer has made an important
contribution to the body of recovery literature."

Milton S. Magness, D.Min.
Author of *Stop Sex Addiction* and *Real Hope, True Freedom*

"A tremendous new resource. Tidwell Palmer's clear
voice combined with well-placed, true-to-life examples
leads readers toward a realistic vision of regained
footing and an action plan that honors one's reality. We
cannot wait to share this book with the spouses and
partners we work with. Thank you Vicki!"

Drs. Bill and Ginger Bercaw, CSATs, CSTs
Authors of *The Couple's Guide to Intimacy* and
From the Living Room to the Bedroom

MOVING BEYOND BETRAYAL

Vicki Tidwell Palmer

MOVING *Beyond* BETRAYAL

The 5-Step Boundary **Solution** for Partners of Sex Addicts

CENTRAL RECOVERY PRESS

LAS VEGAS

Central Recovery Press (CRP) is committed to publishing exceptional materials addressing addiction treatment, recovery, and behavioral healthcare topics.

For more information, visit www.centralrecoverypress.com.

Publisher: Central Recovery Press
            3321 N. Buffalo Drive
            Las Vegas, NV 89129

21 20 19 18 17 16   1 2 3 4 5

Library of Congress Cataloging-in-Publication Data

Names: Palmer, Vicki Tidwell, author.
Title: Moving beyond betrayal : the 5-step boundary solution for partners of
    sex addicts / Vicki Tidwell Palmer.
Description: Las Vegas, NV : Central Recovery Press, 2016. | Description
    based on print version record and CIP data provided by publisher; resource
    not viewed.
Identifiers: LCCN 2016002067 (print) | LCCN 2016000455 (ebook) | ISBN
    9781942094159 (ebook) | ISBN 9781942094142 (paperback)
Subjects: LCSH: Sex addiction. | Sex addicts--Rehabilitation. | Adjustment
    (Psychology) | BISAC: PSYCHOLOGY / Interpersonal Relations. | FAMILY &
    RELATIONSHIPS / Marriage. | PSYCHOLOGY / Psychopathology / Addiction.
Classification: LCC RC560.S43 (print) | LCC RC560.S43 P35 2016 (ebook) | DDC
    616.85/833--dc23
LC record available at http://lccn.loc.gov/2016002067

Photo of Vicki Tidwell Palmer by Rupa Kapoor. Used with permission.

Cover and interior design and layout by Sara Streifel, Think Creative Design

Dedicated to my husband, Micheal

For your courage, perseverance, and grace.
Our relationship has changed the trajectory of my life.

Table of Contents

A Word about Pronouns

Addiction in all its forms does not discriminate on the basis of gender, race, socioeconomic status, sexual orientation, gender identity, or spiritual beliefs—and sex addiction is no exception. There are female sex addicts as well as gay and lesbian sex addicts. There are female partners of sex addicts and there are male partners of sex addicts. While it's true that the majority of people who seek help for sexually compulsive behavior are men, women also suffer from the devastating effects of sex addiction.

When speaking and writing about sex addicts and their partners, the sex addict is almost always referred to as a man, and his partner, wife, or spouse is referred to as a woman. Unfortunately, this heterocentric bias has the unintended consequence of excluding many—female sex addicts, same-sex couples, and others—who don't fit the "norm."

I remember a day in early August 2015 listening to one of my clients in session telling me a story about a friend of hers. She referred to the friend as "married . . . to a man." It was the first time I had ever heard someone specifically state the gender of the person a woman was married to. The June 26, 2015 United States Supreme Court ruling on same-sex marriage has forever altered the way we think, and talk, about marriage and partnering.

In an effort to honor the diversity of marriage and the many faces of intimate partnerships, I originally attempted to vary the pronouns throughout the book by referring to the sex addict as "him" in some chapters while using "her" in others (and vice versa for partners). However, this method led to incongruent or confusing examples of behaviors and scenarios, and generally seemed to do little but distract from the subject at hand. Adding "or her" to every mention of "him," and "or his" to every instance of "hers," seemed just as convoluted. In the end I resolved, for the sake of simplicity, to simply keep with "him" and "his" throughout when referring to the sex addict and to "her" and "hers" when speaking of the partner. I ask the reader to stay cognizant of the fact that what is being said of male sex addicts of course also applies to female ones, and that what is true of female partners is equally applicable to their male counterparts.

Acknowledgments

No creative endeavor is born from the efforts of its creator alone. There are innumerable events and encounters that form the foundation and impulse to bring a book into being, and *Moving Beyond Betrayal* is no exception.

I owe a deep debt of gratitude to Pia Mellody for her practical yet profound teaching on boundaries. Her work has significantly informed my understanding of how boundaries operate in relationships. Pia's persistent appeal to her students to be part of the solution, rather than the problem, has been a guiding principle in my life—both personally and professionally.

I am grateful to have had the opportunity to study and train with many experts in the field of sex addiction treatment including Patrick Carnes, Ken Adams, Stefanie Carnes, Alex Katehakis, and Rob Weiss. And to Kelly McDaniel, for her words of wisdom and encouragement at a chance meeting just a month before the manuscript was due.

Having traveled my own path of recovery for the past twenty-eight years, there are many women and men to whom I offer deep thanks for sharing their experience, strength, and hope. I want to especially thank several key individuals who must remain anonymous, yet have contributed so much to my personal growth and the creation of this book. I am eternally grateful to you.

I also want to thank Lynn Grodzki for her practical and clear-headed guidance, as well as Lisa Tener and Bill O'Hanlon for their expert advice that helped me realize my dream of writing a book. Special thanks to the staff of Central Recovery Press and Eliza Tutellier, my editor.

Lastly, I want to thank my clients—partners and addicts alike—who have trusted me at the most vulnerable and critical times of their lives. Witnessing their transformation and the tenacious resilience of the human spirit is a persistent source of hope, joy, and inspiration to me.

Introduction

"Truth is powerful and it prevails."

—*Sojourner Truth*

The discovery or disclosure that your partner has betrayed you and your relationship in the most intimate way possible—the sexual bond—is devastating. It turns your world upside down and makes you doubt everything you thought you knew about your partner, your relationship, or even yourself. You may doubt your own perceptions and your reality. To choose to stay in a relationship crippled by sexual betrayal and to work through the pain, loss, and uncertainty is no less than heroic, for both the partner and the sex addict.

For more than eight years as a licensed clinical social worker and certified sex addiction therapist, I have worked with partners of sex addicts and sex addicts in individual, group, and couples therapy. I have treated partners in varying stages of their healing journey, beginning with the pre-discovery phase, through the crisis stage, and into the growth and thriving stage. One of the greatest joys of my work is to witness the transformation of my clients. The personal and relational growth that is possible with commitment, perseverance, and hard work is remarkable.

I've seen firsthand the pain and suffering endured by partners of sex addicts caused by lack of information, misinformation, or the absence of good self-care and boundaries. What I know for sure is that if you're in an intimate relationship with someone struggling with out-of-control sexual behavior, you must arm yourself with knowledge and expert guidance.

You may think that if your sex addict partner gets help, all your problems will be solved. I hope to persuade you to adopt another, more powerful mindset. You've been deceived, betrayed, and deeply wounded. These experiences alone warrant a period of focused and deliberate self-care and healing.

There are many residual effects of living with an addict still active in his addiction. Your esteem has likely been eroded over time, impacting the way you feel about yourself physically, sexually, and emotionally. If you've been with your partner for many years, you may have lost respect for yourself, wondering why you're still in the relationship, or why you "put up" with repeated indiscretions and disappointments.

Living with active addiction often means a life of broken promises, empty threats, lies, and other crazy-making experiences. Once surrounded by the fog of addiction, you feel as though you're at the mercy of the addict's unpredictable and chaotic dance. But that is an illusion.

With the tools of the 5-Step Boundary Solution (5-SBS) presented in this book, you will regain your ability to identify and trust your own reality. You will learn how to reclaim your personal power by taking action to get your needs met rather than waiting, wishing, or hoping for the sex addict to stop his behaviors so that you can get on with your life and feel better.

This book is especially helpful if you

• don't know what boundaries are;

• are confused about how to set boundaries;

• aren't sure if you have a right to set boundaries;

• have set boundaries in the past but didn't know what to do when they were violated;

• come from a family where boundaries were frequently violated or nonexistent.

Chapter One, "Your Future Is Not Your Past," starts with the bold promise that even though you've been living in the fog of sex addiction and were profoundly betrayed by the most important person in your life—there is hope. You will learn the ways sex addiction has impacted you, why you've struggled to maintain your reality, and how the 5-SBS can guide you through the process of gaining clarity and finding serenity, by setting and maintaining effective boundaries.

Chapter Two, "Not All Addictions Are Created Equal: What You Need to Know about Sex Addiction," focuses on the basics of addiction and the important differences between sex addiction and other forms of addiction. You may be skeptical about the sex addiction label and wonder if it's just a convenient excuse for bad behavior. This question is addressed, along with an outline of the fundamentals of a good first-year addiction recovery plan for sex addicts.

Chapter Three, "First Things First: How to Recognize a Good Boundary When You See One," discusses our natural and innate urge to seek safety and why boundaries are essential for your healing. You will learn the two functions of boundaries, the use of "non-negotiable" boundaries, along with some of the common boundaries set by partners of sex addicts in the early stages of discovery and/or disclosure.

Chapter Four, "Boundary Solution Step 1: Knowing and Owning Your Reality," shows how being in relationship with an addict has a devastating impact on your ability to know and trust your reality. You will learn specific tools to recognize and honor your innate capacity to recognize your truth so that you can regain trust in your reality and intuition.

In Chapter Five, "Boundary Solution Step 2: Getting Your Needs Met," you will identify the specific needs that aren't currently being met in your life and in your relationship, and you will create a vision for the future. By starting with the end in sight, you'll be better able to recognize the boundaries you need to set.

Chapter Six, "Boundary Solution Step 3: Identifying Your Power Center," focuses on the ways in which powerlessness, authentic personal power, and "power over" manifest in relationships, and how working with power dynamics can enrich or damage your relationship. You will learn the difference between expectations and contracts, and how to use authentic personal power to create an action plan. By owning your power you will avoid the dangers of not taking action, remaining in a victim position, or creating toxic power struggles with the sex addict.

In Chapter Seven, "Boundary Solution Step 4: Creating and Implementing Your Action Plan," you will learn the difference between ultimatums, demands, and requests. You will understand why demands and ultimatums don't work, and why making requests is the most effective way to gain clarity and resolution. You will learn how to make clear, effective requests and what to do when your partner says "no" to a request.

Chapter Eight, "Boundary Solution Step 5: Evaluate Your Results: Mission Accomplished . . . or Not: When Boundaries Are Broken," invites you to take a moment to celebrate if your efforts have been successful, and addresses what to do when boundaries don't work, are broken, or are violated. This is one of the most difficult and challenging aspects of boundary work. You will learn specific steps to take when a boundary violation occurs, along with how to determine an appropriate "repair" when an agreement is broken.

Because broken agreements, boundary violations, and unsuccessful boundary work are a major source of frustration and confusion, you may be tempted to skip ahead and go straight to this chapter. I encourage you, even if you begin with Chapter Eight, to go back to the prior steps of the 5-SBS before attempting to fix any boundaries with which you're currently struggling. Laying the foundation for your boundary work—through 1) knowing your reality, 2) knowing your needs and wants, 3) identifying where you have power (or don't), and 4) how to take effective and meaningful action—will save you time, effort, and heartache.

Chapter Nine, "Speed Bumps, Roadblocks, and Crash Landings: Hidden Barriers to Boundary Work and What to Do about Them," discusses why, even with guidance, good intentions, and support, partners sometimes struggle to follow through with boundary work. This can happen for a variety of reasons including not feeling good enough, difficulty managing emotions, financial considerations, or pre-relationship trauma. Regardless of the reasons, identifying where the challenges are—and knowing what to do about them—will help you make course corrections and lay the groundwork for a more successful outcome the next time around.

Chapter Ten, "Burning Is Learning: How Your New Boundary Muscle Will Keep You Strong and Serene for a Lifetime," shows you how the skills and tools you'll learn in this book are indispensable not only in your current situation, but in all areas of your life. Once you understand the fundamentals of good boundary work, you can apply them in any setting or situation—with extended family relationships, friends, coworkers, employers, children, and many more. Mastering boundaries also has a powerful lasting impact on your confidence and self-esteem.

The last chapter, Chapter Eleven, "Partners Beyond Betrayal: Trust, Gratitude, and Forgiveness," discusses three central themes of partners' healing from the impact of sex addiction after the discovery and crisis stage. Fair warning: this chapter is not for the faint of heart. Arriving at trust, gratitude, and forgiveness are monumental steps for partners, and they come in their own time. You will hear from real partners who have traveled the courageous journey to find a new and better way of living than they ever imagined. These partners have truly moved beyond betrayal.

In order to get the most out of this book and quickly learn the five steps of the 5-Step Boundary Solution process, I recommend that you go online now, before continuing to read, and download the free "5-SBS Clarifier" at www.vickitidwellpalmer.com/5sbsclarifier.

The "Clarifier" is a two-page worksheet outlining each of the five steps of the 5-SBS process with brief instructions for each step. Use one "Clarifier" for each boundary you would like to create or for boundaries that have been broken or violated.

At the end of Chapters Four through Eight there are exercises that guide you through completing each of the respective steps in the 5-SBS process. Use the "5-SBS Clarifier" you downloaded to record your answers and reflections for each step as you work through them.

For the purpose of learning the 5-SBS process, as you go through the steps outlined in each chapter, I suggest you choose one relatively simple problem you believe may require a boundary, or a known boundary you want to create, that may or may not be related to your partner. For example, you may have a friend who is consistently late for social events or a family member who occasionally tries to tell you what to do or how to parent your children. Whatever the issue, choose one that has a relatively low level of importance to you and answer the questions for each step based on the issue you chose. This will help you move through the

5-SBS process with greater ease as you're learning how to tackle more serious and complex boundary problems.

While the information and tools presented here are specifically designed for both current and former partners of sex addicts, the concepts and step-by-step instructions of the 5-SBS can be applied to relationships with addicts of all kinds, with difficult people in general, and in any relationship with boundary challenges. The fundamentals of boundary work are universal, applicable, and effective in all relationships.

Some readers—especially those with experience in psychotherapy or twelve-step programs—may find they already have a good grasp of one or more of the steps in the 5-SBS. If that is the case for you, congratulations! While some of the concepts may be familiar, I still recommend that you review each step before you proceed to the next one, even if you feel you have a good grasp of the concept already. In my experience, most people struggle with at least two of the steps as they navigate through their boundary work.

Partners, in spite of everything you've been through, you can survive and thrive after sexual betrayal. It's not an easy road, and it's not a short journey. But with knowledge, self-care, and boundaries, it is possible to move beyond the despair and pain of discovery to find clarity and serenity.

Let's get started.

CHAPTER ONE

Your Future Is Not Your Past

"Even though the future seems far away,
it is actually beginning right now."

—*Mattie Stepanek*

THE COURAGEOUS JOURNEY

If you've taken the courageous step of picking up this book, you're probably in a relationship with a sex addict, you know someone who is, or you're the former partner of an addict. Perhaps you're a sex addict yourself.

If you're an addict and you've picked up this book because you're skeptical or worried about what I might recommend to your partner, I ask that you trust the process—just like you're asking her to trust the process of your own healing and recovery. Although you may not like everything you read here, this book will help your partner take care of herself. Practicing good self-care will help her feel better, and when she feels better your relationship will improve—provided you're engaged in your own healing and recovery work.

If both of you want to stay together and you're both willing to put the time and energy into your work—individually and as a couple—there is a very high likelihood you will make it. Having worked with many couples who have experienced sexual betrayal over the years, I have never seen one I thought couldn't salvage their relationship if they both did the necessary work.

As a partner of a sex addict, you may not know where to begin and you may be confused about what to do. The 5-SBS will help you navigate through the painful first year after discovery or disclosure of your partner's sex addiction, and beyond. You will learn what a sound sexual recovery plan looks like and know your rights as a partner. You will also learn the fundamentals of good boundary work that I refer to as the ultimate self-care practice. When facing a condition as serious as sex addiction, the practice of self-care through good boundary work can change the course of your life and your relationships.

THE TRANSFORMATIONAL POWER OF BOUNDARIES

When I say that practicing self-care through good boundaries can change your life and your relationships, I speak from personal experience. Boundary work saved my marriage of twenty-nine years. More than a decade ago, after many years of individual therapy and intermittent couples work, I reached the end of the proverbial rope in my marriage. At the suggestion of the therapist I was seeing at the time, I decided I needed a thirty-day therapeutic separation[1] from my husband. I realized I couldn't keep doing the same things and expecting different results. Separation seemed like the next logical step. I didn't want a divorce, but I couldn't live any longer in the marriage as it was.

---

[1] Therapeutic separation is a planned period of time for the couple to focus on individual work, learn new skills, reevaluate the relationship, and potentially recommit with healthier boundaries and agreements.

The day I decided to tell my husband I wanted a separation happened to be a Friday. Little did I know that my resolve would be immediately tested. When you express a limit (also known as a boundary) to someone, it must come from a place of clarity and commitment. If emotions are running high, you'll be tempted to make threats and issue ultimatums. The problem is that ultimatums and threats are almost always hollow because they're not grounded on a firm foundation. When requests and boundaries are based on a foundation of clarity and personal authentic power (more on that in Chapter Six), you will be unshakable. You will feel calm in the midst of the storm.

When I told my husband I wanted a thirty-day separation I was unshakable. He attempted to buy time and perhaps convince me to change my mind. He told me he was fine with leaving but he wanted to wait until Sunday. Without skipping a beat, I told him he could stay in our home until Sunday, but that I would be leaving that day with our son to stay in a hotel until he left. Had I not been clear and resolved I might have gone along with his request or gotten into a power struggle with him about who was going to leave.

Countless times I've heard partners ask questions like, "Why should I have to _____ (leave the family home, take a time-out, get tested for sexually transmitted infections)?" Although the frustration is understandable—after all, you didn't cause the breach in trust—the truth is that you're the only person you have control over. When you lose focus on your goal and engage in power struggles, you're stuck in the victim role, and caught up in attempting to use control versus doing good boundary work.

As you will learn, one of the ways you'll know when a boundary you've set is right for you is when you feel a calm, grounded resolve even in the face of pushback, resistance, or outright hostility. You will know by how you feel that it's right. And that's exactly how I felt in that moment.

That fateful day was a turning point in our marriage. It wasn't the end of conflict or disappointment—those are part of being in any relationship. But it marked a fundamental shift in me and in the relationship that has lasted to this day. Of course, it also required a commitment from him to his own personal growth, and to our marriage.

> The effective use of boundaries is one of the best ways to determine whether or not your relationship is salvageable.

In my case it was. However, if my husband had made different choices I would have gotten the information I needed to decide whether or not I wanted to remain in the marriage. One of the gifts of good boundary work is that it enables you to see your own limits and the limits of others. You learn how far you're willing to go with others and how far they're willing to go with you. When you're clear about these two things, you avoid wasting time in relationships that aren't healthy or fulfilling.

My request for a thirty-day separation wasn't about threats, manipulation, punishment, ultimatums, or the many other ineffective ways we attempt to get what we want and need in relationships. My request was about reaching a limit and knowing what I needed to do to take care of me.

> Limits are boundaries, and boundaries are self-care. I would even go so far as to say that boundaries are an act of self-love.

THE FOG OF ADDICTION

If you're in a relationship with a sex addict who's still acting out or is in early recovery, your life and relationship are in crisis. It's likely you've been repeatedly lied to, manipulated, or "gaslighted." Gaslighting is a term often used to describe one of the ways addicts avoid being found out. It's a form of psychological manipulation intended to cause you to question your own sanity. For example, your partner may tell you that you didn't hear what you know you heard, or that he said something that you're sure he didn't say. If these deceptive incidents repeat with regularity, you eventually lose faith in your ability to know what is real and what isn't.

As a partner, you may have even been overtly abused— verbally, physically, or sexually. Your life may be drama-filled and chaotic. Your relationship may feel like it's about to end, and you may wonder why you're still in it. Living in the chaos and fog of addiction creates immense pain, suffering, loss of esteem, and undeserved consequences related to the addict's behavior.

You may live in a constant state of anxiety and feel fundamentally unsafe in the world. Partners often experience panic episodes before and during discovery or disclosure. If you have children, you may worry about how or whether they've been impacted by the addict's behaviors, or how they've been affected by living in a family where active addiction is present.

As a partner (or former partner) of a sex addict, you may have attempted to change the addict's behavior or get him help in various ways. He may have told you he stopped, or that he would stop after a certain time, or that he would get help . . . but he didn't follow through. You've probably made threats or issued ultimatums to the sex addict for continuing his behavior—threats on which you didn't follow through. There have likely been broken agreements and promises that left you feeling helpless or powerless.

You want him to stop his self-destructive and relationship-destroying behaviors and you wonder why he can't. You may have thought that if he loved you, he could—or would—stop hurting you so much. Sadly, when it comes to addiction "just do it" just doesn't work.

I want you to understand how vulnerable you are when you take the perspective that when he stops or gets better you'll feel better. I want you to recognize and own the power you have now, in this moment, to begin the process of healing and eventually thriving—with or without the sex addict in your life. With the skills and tools in this book, you will learn the power that comes from focusing on you, on your needs and wants, learning how to make requests when that's appropriate, and what to do when boundaries are broken. The bad news is the sex addict's out-of-control behavior and what it has done to you. The good news—and the solution to your pain—lies with you. You may have been a victim of his deception and betrayal, but you are no longer a victim. You have the power to take charge of your life beginning right now.

Knowledge is power, and this is especially true when it comes to breaking through the fog and pain of being in relationship with a sex addict. This book will give you, as a partner or former partner, the information you need about sex addiction and sex addiction recovery so that you can make informed and effective choices in your best interest.

Even if you've had prior experiences in relationships with addicts of other kinds, don't expect to use the same skill set and strategies with the sex addict in your life. There are fundamental differences between sex addiction and alcohol or other drug addictions, both in the recovery process and in the issues partners face. You will save yourself time and heartache by knowing the difference.

PARTNERS OF SEX ADDICTS: CO-ADDICTS OR TRAUMA SURVIVORS?

In the early days of sex addiction treatment, the focus was primarily on the sex addict. Most of the literature available, as well as the treatment models used, were geared toward helping the addict establish a solid foundation in recovery. For the most part, the partner of the addict was on her own either with no support or sometimes with a therapist who had little information about sex addiction or worked with the partner from a co-addiction or codependency model.

Al-Anon, the twelve-step program founded in 1951 by Lois W. (wife of Bill W., the founder of Alcoholics Anonymous), is based on a co-addict/codependency model. The co-addiction model says that partners of addicts play a role in the addiction cycle by refusing to acknowledge that the addict has a problem (denial), by enabling the addict's behaviors, or by using various strategies to control the addict's behaviors, either directly or indirectly. Al-Anon is a helpful program and I often refer clients to it. However, the co-addiction model doesn't address the special circumstances and needs of partners of sex addicts. This perspective often leaves partners feeling that they're at fault for the addict's behavior.

Most partners see themselves as profoundly defective and inadequate after the discovery of extramarital affairs, anonymous sex, or the compulsive use of pornography. You may believe that if you were like the women (or men) in the pornography your sex addict partner looks at or like the person he had an affair with — he wouldn't have strayed. Or maybe if you had just gone along with some of the sexual activities he wanted to do that didn't feel comfortable to you, he wouldn't have been unfaithful.

Although none of these provide an explanation for the addict's behaviors, it's logical and understandable for you to think his sexual indiscretions are about you. When your partner chooses another person or pornography over being sexual with you, the experience and the impact is much different from finding out he's been secretly gambling or using drugs. The sex addict's behavior is felt on a deeply personal level that affects you in ways other addictive behaviors don't. In Chapter Two I offer more detail about how the experience of partners of sex addicts differs from that of partners of all other addicts due to the intimate nature of sexual betrayal.

Most sex addicts avoid emotional, physical, and sexual intimacy with their partners. This is not because they aren't attracted to their partner or because they think she's lacking in some way. In fact, sex addicts often can't understand why they engage in behaviors that cause them to risk losing someone they deeply love and to whom they are sexually attracted. This is one of the reasons I was not in favor of the term "Hypersexual Disorder" as a description for sex addiction or out-of-control sexual behavior as it was proposed for the most recent version of the *Diagnostic and Statistical Manual of Mental Disorders (DSM)*. In my experience working with sex addicts and their partners, the majority of sex addicts are sexual with their partners far less frequently than they are outside the relationship. Although it's beyond the scope of this book to address how sex addiction develops, it is often the result of co-occurring mental health issues and/or trauma.

Because of the personal nature of sexual betrayal, you may not relate to the co-addict approach that emphasizes the partner's role in the addictive dance. You may feel responsible or blamed for the addict's behavior. Although it's true that partners can exhibit codependent behaviors and play a role in a dysfunctional relationship dynamic, you are not responsible in any way for the sex addict's choices.

Thanks to the work of many in the field of sex addiction treatment, we now have a better understanding of how to address the needs of partners. The most immediate need is to assess the level of trauma you've experienced. Many partners suffer from symptoms of Post-Traumatic Stress Disorder (PTSD)—the most common being panic episodes, distressing memories, and intrusive thoughts about discovery and/or disclosure, sleep problems, or feeling perpetually on guard and anxious. Some partners have symptoms that rise to the level of a formal PTSD diagnosis. The partner's trauma is brought on by the addict's lies, deception, and gaslighting, which are discussed in greater detail in Chapter Four.

First and foremost, partners must be heard and validated. Depending on the severity of the trauma symptoms you're experiencing, you may need trauma-specific treatment such as Somatic Experiencing (SE), Eye Movement Desensitization and Reprocessing Therapy (EMDR), or Sensorimotor Psychotherapy. If your symptoms are worse, a multi-day workshop or inpatient treatment may be needed. (See Appendix for treatment resources.)

Once past the initial crisis stage, family of origin issues or other childhood trauma may need to be addressed before you can fully deal with the current relational trauma, especially if you were a victim of childhood sexual abuse or if there was active sex addiction in your family of origin. A partner's unresolved childhood trauma can render her unable to do the necessary self-care and boundary work in her current relationship that is so important for her healing.

Ideally, the partner's trauma, as well as any codependency issues, needs to be addressed. I believe it's a mistake to dismiss either the trauma approach or potential issues of codependency as invalid or irrelevant. If codependency issues aren't addressed, you may ask too little of the sex addict or accept halfhearted and superficial efforts at recovery. You also may be vulnerable to discounting or ignoring your needs, especially if the sex addict is highly defensive or, worse, a bully. The reality is that most partners experience trauma symptoms as a result of discovery/disclosure. In addition, they often have participated in some way in the dysfunctional addictive system, if only by neglecting their own needs or being unable to speak their truth.

THE WAY OUT

This book offers concrete tips, tools, and skills to help you navigate through this painful and difficult time in your life and regain trust in your intuition. You will learn:

- How to use the 5-SBS to practice exquisite self-care through effective boundary work;

- How to tap into your authentic power and stop using ineffective strategies of control and manipulation;

- How to set boundaries;

- What to do when boundaries you set are violated; and

- How to determine whether or not your relationship is salvageable.

You will also come to realize that, although you don't have the power to change your partner, you do have the power to change how you navigate this difficult phase and your relationship. You can reduce the chaos in your life, gain clarity, and ultimately experience serenity.

One of the most powerful lessons you will learn is that self-care and boundary work will change your relationships forever—with your partner, family, friends, coworkers, or children. Waiting for someone else to change is a losing proposition. Changing yourself is in your power and you can start immediately.

Here's a snapshot of the 5-SBS for creating and maintaining good, healthy boundaries:

1. Define your current problem(s) through knowing your reality.

2. Identify the needs that aren't being met and create a vision for the future.

3. Identify where you have power.

4. Take action where you have the power to effect change.

5. Evaluate the results to determine if your goal has been accomplished or further boundary work is needed.

Of course, there are times when our best efforts fail and that is certainly true for boundaries. Broken agreements, boundary violations, and a host of other factors can get in the way. You will learn how to handle boundary violations and learn what to do about any personal challenges that are sabotaging your boundary work.

My sincere desire is that the information and tools presented in this book will give you hope, help you develop a better relationship with yourself and the sex addict in your life, and guide you in creating the life you want and deserve.

CHAPTER TWO

Not All Forms of Addiction Are Created Equal: What You Need to Know about Sex Addiction

THE ABCS OF ADDICTION

Addiction is a pernicious, crippling, lifelong condition. Addiction is deadly and has an arsenal of means with which to kill. The actor Philip Seymour Hoffman was found dead in early 2014 in his apartment with a needle in his arm—the result of a heroin overdose. It would be more accurate to say that he committed suicide. He had relapsed about a year earlier after twenty-three years in recovery. One of the many problems with addiction is that when you relapse, you don't start over as a first-time user. You start where you left off.

According to the American Society of Addiction Medicine (ASAM), addiction is characterized by "an inability to consistently abstain, impairment in behavior control, craving, diminished recognition of significant problems with one's behaviors and interpersonal relationships, and a dysfunctional emotional response." The "inability to consistently abstain" is a concept that sometimes confuses loved ones and family members close to the addict. They wonder, "How is it possible for the addict to abstain if addiction means that's something they can't do?" The confusion is understandable. On their own, addicts lack the ability to consistently abstain *without help*. Most would stop their compulsive behaviors on their own if they could. It's just that most can't do it alone.

An addict's inability to consistently abstain or practice behavioral control manifests in many ways. He may make promises to himself that he won't engage in a particular behavior again or he may tell himself that after a certain date in the future he'll quit. Of course, these promises are rarely kept.

The craving for the addictive substance or behavior grows over time and the addict needs more to get the same effect. If he's an alcoholic, he will require more alcohol to get the same level of intoxication. In sex addiction, the addict may increase the time spent engaged in a particular sexual behavior over time, or engage in increasingly risky behaviors to get the same level of intensity or "high." "Acting out" is a commonly used expression to describe the addict's compulsive behaviors.

Because of an inability to recognize the extent of the problems related to their behavior, addicts usually experience serious life consequences. They have chronic feelings of low self-worth and shame due to the secret double lives they lead. They often suffer from underperforming at work due to preoccupation with the substance or behavior, or a "hangover" effect from having recently acted out or binged. They may even lose their jobs because of poor performance or violating company policies. Addicts suffer financially because of work-related issues or spending large sums of money on the addictive substance or behavior. Some addicts manage to avoid financial or career consequences—but their close, intimate relationships are almost always negatively impacted.

There are two primary forms of addiction: substance addiction and process addiction. Substance addiction includes alcohol, prescription medications, and/or illegal drugs. Process addiction is different from substance addiction because it involves a set of behaviors rather than the ingestion of a substance. Examples of process addictions include gambling, food disorders, and sex addiction. In many ways, process addiction (especially food disorders and sex addiction) is more challenging to overcome because it involves normal, healthy activities, when done in moderation. In alcohol and other drug addiction treatment, abstinence is defined as simply stopping the consumption of the substance in question. However, it's not realistic to abstain from food or to choose not to be sexual for the remainder of one's life.

Addiction is considered a lifelong, chronic issue similar to medical conditions that require sustained and continuous behavior modification. There is general consensus among mental health and other professionals who work in the field that addiction is never "cured." However, addiction can be well managed with guidance and support, usually in the form of counseling, psychotherapy, twelve-step groups, and—in more serious cases—inpatient treatment.

WHAT SETS SEX ADDICTION APART

Today's misconceptions about sex addiction are sadly similar to how people thought of alcoholics in the 1930s and 1940s. At that time, the common view was that if you were a "real" alcoholic you would be homeless and lying in a gutter somewhere. We now know that many high-functioning people can lead what appears to be a normal life while active in their addiction—whether to alcohol, other drugs, gambling, or sex.

The addict's recovery process and the ways in which sex addiction impacts partners are different from other forms of addiction. Five major factors distinguish sex addiction discovery and recovery:

1. *Sexual betrayal is experienced as a personal assault by the partner.* If the addict in your life abuses alcohol and other drugs you may be frustrated and angry about his behavior. You may even be hurt by the thought that he seems to care more about alcohol than he does about you. On the other hand, if the addict spends hours a day looking at pornography, frequenting adult bookstores, having affairs, or hiring prostitutes for sex, the level of betrayal and hurt experienced is multiplied exponentially.

2. *Sexual betrayal creates serious health risks for partners.* If a sex addict has unprotected sex with anyone other than his partner and hides this information from her, the consequences may be deadly. The risk is compounded by the fact that she isn't aware that she may have been exposed to a sexually transmitted infection and/or disease.

3. *Abstinence from sex is not the goal.* For most forms of addiction, the simple (but not necessarily easy) solution is to abstain from the substance or the behavior. Defining abstinence in sex addiction is more complex because sex is a pleasurable and evolutionarily desirable behavior fundamental to human existence.

4. *Slips and relapses are often more common in sex addiction recovery.* This is difficult for partners to accept, and rightfully so. But the truth is that, for a variety of reasons, people who attempt to replace compulsive sexual behavior with healthy sex generally aren't able to simply make a decision to stop all unhealthy sexual patterns and never repeat them. The addict's sobriety plan may change over time depending on his particular set of behaviors and issues. There can be several—or even many—setbacks along the way. Depending on the behaviors involved, these "slips" may be deal-breakers for partners.

5. *Need for more intensive accountability.* If your partner is drinking or using other drugs, it's hard not to notice even if he's a master at avoiding detection. The odors and/or unusual behaviors of people when they're using substances are difficult to miss. However, it's entirely possible for someone to engage in sexual behaviors either alone or with another person during the lunch hour, on the way home from work, while running errands on the weekend, or at home in the middle of the night, without any evidence or clues. This is one of the reasons why formal therapeutic disclosure followed by a polygraph exam has become common in sex addiction recovery. For people who haven't had experience with a sexually compulsive partner, these accountability measures may sound extreme. However, it's not unusual for a recovering drug addict to be required to pass a sobriety test (such as urinalysis, breathalyzer, or a hair follicle test) in order to have visitation with children, for example. The polygraph is the equivalent of the drug test as an accountability tool to repair the damage done in relationships impacted by compulsive sexual behavior.

THE SEX ADDICTION "EXCUSE"

Partners who have recently discovered that their spouse has been acting out sexually sometimes say, "He says he's a sex addict, but I think it's an excuse. He's just trying to avoid responsibility by claiming it's an addiction." The idea is that somehow the "sex addict" label lets him off the hook, renders him not responsible in some way, or gives him license to get away with something. I want to assure you that nothing could be further from the truth.

Sex addiction is real. The risks taken by sex addicts that endanger their health, safety, livelihood, and relationships are staggering. Addicts look for anonymous sexual partners through websites, chat rooms, and phone apps; they meet people they don't know in risky or even dangerous places, and have unprotected sex with people whose sexual history is completely unknown. They may literally risk their lives for the next sexual encounter.

Partners sometimes believe that when the sex addict is acting out he is sneaking around like an adolescent whose parents are out of town, having casual hookups or engaging in other behaviors that he experiences as merely fun and harmless. Addicts often minimize their behaviors or say that what they did "meant nothing" in an attempt to avoid consequences or manage their shame. Addiction is not casual, fun, or harmless. The level of preoccupation, desperation, unmanageability, and shame experienced by sex addicts is so painful that they create distinct "compartments" to manage their dark, secret life.

No one would willingly choose to be an addict—especially a sex addict. It is difficult enough for most people to talk about healthy sexuality, much less to admit to out-of-control sexual behavior. Taking on the sex addict label—with all the work it entails—requires a considerable commitment of time, energy, and dedication. In addition to counseling and twelve-step meetings, the addict may be asked to write a formal disclosure to present to his partner, followed by a polygraph exam.

Given all that's involved in taking on the sex addict label, it's clearly not an excuse for bad behavior or a way to avoid responsibility. Quite the contrary. A person who identifies as a sex addict and makes a decision to get help to stop his behaviors is making a long-term—often lifelong—commitment to treatment and recovery.

BASICS OF FIRST-YEAR SEX ADDICTION RECOVERY

As a partner, you need to have an understanding of the addiction recovery process in order to develop realistic expectations and to make informed, reasonable requests of the addict as necessary.

Otherwise, you will experience needless frustration because your expectations of your partner are unrealistic, or worse, you may expect and ask for too little. Being uninformed and/or not making requests of the addict for trust-building behaviors is harmful not only to you but it may also inadvertently delay the recovery process for the sex addict.

The truth is that most of us don't make meaningful changes without engaging in behaviors and activities outside our comfort zone. While it's not your job as a partner to provide the addict with growth opportunities, you'll be doing yourself and your relationship a disservice by not making requests for repair and rehabilitation of trust. In Chapters Three, Six, and Seven, you'll learn about common boundaries made by partners and how to make effective requests of the sex addict in your life.

Following are the primary components of a good first-year sexual recovery plan. These are the typical recommendations Certified Sex Addiction Therapists (CSATs) make, and may not represent the treatment approach of other mental health treatment providers or recovery programs.

- Assessment by a mental health professional with specialized training in treating compulsive sexual behavior. The International Institute for Trauma and Addiction Professionals (IITAP) and the Society for the Advancement of Sexual Health (SASH) are good resources for locating a certified sex addiction therapist or a therapist with specialized training and experience (see Appendix for more information). Mental health professionals without knowledge or training about compulsive sexual behavior sometimes don't know how to assess the problem, and they can overlook or minimize it. Most sex addicts minimize the extent of their problematic behaviors. On the other hand, some people who are deeply troubled by their sexual behaviors and those who experience intense shame about normal sexual feelings or behaviors may label themselves as sex addicts when it's simply not the case. That's why assessment is so important.

• Participation in regular (preferably weekly) individual and group psychotherapy, along with attending twelve-step meetings, and working with a twelve-step sponsor. Sponsors are mentors in twelve-step programs who serve as guides in the recovery process. (The Appendix includes a list of twelve-step organizations.)

• Therapists and/or sponsors often recommend that addicts new to the recovery process abstain from all sexual behaviors for the first three months of treatment and attend ninety twelve-step meetings in ninety days— sometimes referred to as "ninety in ninety." Although "ninety in ninety" may seem extreme at first glance, when compared to the amount of time many sex addicts spend thinking about, planning, preparing for, and engaging in their sexual behaviors, seven hours a week spent in twelve-step meetings is usually a fraction of the time spent on acting-out behaviors.

• Daily written recovery work and reading of recovery literature.

• Creation of a sex plan or *Three Circle Plan*. This plan outlines the behaviors the addict will abstain from, as well as healthy behaviors that will replace those that are destructive and unhealthy. The behaviors in a sex addict's abstinence plan often change over time. (For more information about the Sex Addicts Anonymous *Three Circle Plan*, visit their website at www.saa-recovery.org.)

• If the sex addict is in a long-term relationship, the partner or therapist may ask him to prepare a formal therapeutic disclosure. The formal disclosure is a document describing the type and extent of his sexual behaviors outside his primary relationship. Graphic details aren't included, but the number of partners, how long the relationship or behavior lasted, and how much money was spent, are typical items included in a disclosure. If he agrees, the sex addict will complete a written disclosure to present to his partner in a therapy session, followed by a polygraph exam. It is sometimes recommended that the sex addict complete the First Step in his twelve-step community before presenting a disclosure to his partner.

Most partners find it helpful to get more information about sex addiction and the recovery process from trusted sources. (See the Appendix for a list of recommended reading.)

RECOVERY "SLIPS" AND RELAPSES

One of the most painful aspects of sex addiction recovery for partners is that the sex addict will likely not be able to put an end to all acting-out behaviors immediately after getting caught, attending his first twelve-step meeting, or beginning therapy. When addicts break their abstinence plan, it's called a slip or a relapse. In an ideal world, addicts would choose sobriety, commit to a recovery path, and remain abstinent from their destructive sexual behaviors for life. Unfortunately, this is rarely the case. More often than not, sex addicts in early recovery struggle to maintain an abstinence plan.

There are differing views about slips and relapses in sex addiction recovery. Most therapists who treat sex addiction agree that a slip is a single—usually unplanned—acting-out incident. Relapse is a process that begins before the actual acting-out behaviors. It may start with a reduction in participation in recovery activities (twelve-step meetings, therapy, etc.), the addict thinking he doesn't need recovery, that his problems aren't as bad as others, or harboring secret plans to engage in what are commonly called the "middle circle" behaviors of the *Three Circle Plan*. Middle circle behaviors are activities that aren't a violation of the abstinence plan, but they have the potential to lead to acting out. Some examples of middle circle behaviors are unstructured alone time, using a computer in isolated circumstances, and traveling out of town for business without one's partner.

Relapses almost always involve deception because the addict, either consciously or unconsciously, knows he's headed down a dangerous path. Once he's acted out, he will rationalize continuing the behaviors even for a short time since he's already violated his abstinence plan. Sadly, addicts sometimes consciously choose to act out prior to a particular milestone of abstinence (sixty or ninety days, for example) because they tell themselves that the disappointment over "failing" after sixty or ninety days would feel worse to them and their partner after reaching the milestone. This is a clear and painful example of the cunning and baffling nature of addictive thinking.

Individuals with sobriety in other twelve-step programs like Alcoholics Anonymous (AA) or Narcotics Anonymous (NA) sometimes criticize the sex addiction recovery community for being too tolerant of slips and relapses. The idea is that in AA or other twelve-step programs, people get sober from the beginning of their time in the program. This is simply not the case. Substance addicts may slip or relapse multiple times over many years before getting a foothold in solid, long-term recovery—sometimes referred to as "rehearsing" sobriety. The story of Bill W., founder of AA, is probably the best, and most well known, example of the reality that sobriety is not a simple onetime choice of abstinence.

Because abstinence in sex addiction recovery isn't as black and white as in alcohol and other drug addiction, it is not uncommon for the definition of abstinence to change, especially in the first year. For example, addicts often complete ninety days of celibacy from all sexual activity in early recovery. During this time, masturbation is considered acting out. However, after the ninety days of abstinence is complete, masturbation may no longer be considered a slip. This is one among many reasons why abstinence in sex addiction is more complicated than other addictions.

HOW PARTNERS ARE IMPACTED

Sex addiction, like all other forms of addiction, involves a considerable amount of isolation and secretiveness on the part of the addict. The isolation inherent in addiction results in frequent deception and lying to partners, family, friends, and employers. As a partner of a sex addict, you need to know that, because of the nature of deception and secrecy that goes hand in hand with addiction, your trust in your reality has likely been seriously impacted.

You may have been told:

- "You're crazy."

- "Why are you so upset? I only did it once."

- "You're overreacting."

- "All men _____ (look at pornography, go to strip clubs, etc.)."

- "You're wrong. You don't know what you're talking about."

These attempts to convince you that you're crazy, stupid, or just plain wrong are what we call gaslighting. The term comes from a 1944 movie called *Gaslight* and, as mentioned before, it denotes a form of mental abuse where the victim is lied to—or the truth is otherwise distorted—for the purpose of causing the victim to doubt her own reality, memory, or perceptions. Gaslighting creates the fog of addiction, and perfectly describes what happens to partners of sex addicts when the addict is still acting out and attempting to cover up his behaviors.

Having been in a relationship with an active addict, your reality has been manipulated. You may not trust your intuition or perceptions. Some addicts are so deceptive, and their lives so Jekyll and Hyde, their partners wonder if they are sociopaths. Of course, it's possible that your partner is a sociopath—but it's unlikely. Many addicts manifest sociopathic characteristics when they're acting out. They use every means available to deceive and cover up the truth of their secret life. The addiction becomes more important than anything else for them, and the level of deception inherent in addiction takes a serious toll on partners.

Some well-meaning but misinformed therapists have encouraged the partner of a sex addict to participate in the acting-out behaviors of the addict even when those behaviors are outside the partner's value system or just aren't something the partner wants to do. These harmful experiences happen too often and delay the addict and partner from getting the help they need. I highly recommend you seek out a professional who is trained in the field of sex addiction treatment and recovery. Don't be afraid to ask detailed questions about the therapist's training, experience, approach to treatment, and any concerns you have.

Because of the level of shame and stigma inherent in sex addiction, you may find it difficult to talk to family or friends about what's going on with you and your partner. It is wise to carefully consider with whom you share information. Because sex addiction is not widely understood, the input and advice you receive may cause more harm than good. Be especially aware of people who immediately tell you to leave or say things like, "I can't believe you're still with him," or "I didn't think you would put up with behavior like that." This kind of advice and feedback is not supportive and actually harmful. You may choose to leave, but you likely have a huge investment of time in the relationship, and perhaps children to consider. Your best course of action is to find a therapist, join a support group or twelve-step community, educate yourself about your situation, and practice the very best self-care you can.

YOUR SELF-CARE IN EARLY DISCOVERY

In the early stages of discovery and disclosure, your world has been turned upside down and—in many ways—shattered. Your brain is trying to assimilate, organize, and comprehend all the incoming data that doesn't correspond to the way you saw your life, your relationship, or your family pre-discovery. You may spend much of your day asking your sex addict partner for information and details about his acting out or engaging in some form of detective work—combing through credit card or bank statements, phone records, or email accounts. You may have even gone a step further and installed keystroke logger software on a computer or phone, or a GPS tracker on your partner's vehicle.

It is completely understandable for you to want to use all means to seek safety through gathering information that has been systematically and deceptively withheld from you. If the sex addict in your life seeks professional help from someone knowledgeable about sex addiction treatment and recovery, he will be given the tools and guidance to prepare a formal disclosure to give you all of the information you want and deserve, followed up by a post-disclosure polygraph if you request one.

As understandable as it is for you to seek safety through gathering information, this will not be your greatest strategy for creating safety. Your greatest source of strength and safety comes from your practice of good self-care through the use of effective boundaries—knowing how they work, how to create them, and what to do when they're broken.

In the next chapter we explore the concept of boundaries and how to recognize a good one when you see it. But first, let's look at the basics of your self-care plan as you navigate this difficult time.

A simple way to think about the primary components of your self-care is the PIES model:

P   Physical

I   Intellectual

E   Emotional

S   Spiritual

Following are examples of how partners practice self-care using this model.

Physical

STI Testing—Even if you don't believe your partner has had sexual contact with another person, you need to be tested for sexually transmitted infections/diseases. Some partners tell me they don't see why they should be tested, either because the sex addict has already been tested or because they don't believe they should have to go through the embarrassment of a visit to the family physician since they didn't do anything wrong. The reality is that regardless of what your partner has done, you are ultimately responsible for your own physical health and well-being. If you're uncomfortable going to your regular physician, consider going to one of the many high-quality community clinics that offer anonymous, low-cost STI testing.

Safe Sex Practices—I am always concerned when a partner tells me she's having unprotected sex with the sex addict after discovery and before the formal disclosure process. Even if you don't believe your partner has been sexual with anyone else, you owe it to yourself to use safe sex practices each and every time until you have more information about the addict's behaviors.

Intellectual

Knowledge is power. Partners should read a variety of books about sex addiction or those specifically written for partners of sex addicts. In addition to gathering information, you will save time and valuable resources by going to a sex addiction specialist first. I've heard many unfortunate stories of couples going to therapists who weren't knowledgeable about sex addiction and offered advice like, "Just go to Victoria's Secret and buy some new lingerie," or "All men _____ (fill in the blank)," and worse.

Emotional

One of the most difficult realities of dealing with the aftermath of discovery is that the person you used to go to for comfort and reassurance has become the person who feels the least trustworthy to you. The sad truth is that even before discovery, your relationship was not as intimate and close as you may have believed. Addicts who are still acting out or who have recently sought help are generally not emotionally available to provide the kind of support, validation, and empathy you need.

Over time, and with healing, the sex addict will become more present and emotionally available. However, in the beginning, you will benefit from finding other sources of emotional connection. Trusted friends, communities of support, and therapy will be your lifelines as you deal with feelings of isolation and uncertainty about whom you can talk to.

Spiritual

Now, more than ever, you need spiritual support and guidance. Spiritual practice can be as simple as spending time in nature, reading inspirational books, or listening to audio programs that bring you a sense of comfort, hope, and peace. If you belong to a church, synagogue, temple, or mosque, I encourage you to attend regularly if your spiritual home is a place of strength, support, and comfort to you. If your spiritual life has been dormant, this is a great time to explore spiritual practices that resonate with you, or religious communities you've been curious about.

Now that you have a good understanding of the sex addiction recovery process and a foundation for your self-care plan, let's take a look at the basics of boundaries.

CHAPTER THREE

First Things First: How to Recognize a Good Boundary When You See One

"Boundaries are to protect life,
not to limit pleasures."

—*Edwin Louis Cole*

THE HUMAN URGE TOWARD SAFETY

One of the most basic human needs is safety. In 1943, Abraham Maslow proposed a theory he called the "Hierarchy of Needs" that has become one of the most widely used theories on human needs. Maslow proposed that all human needs fall into one of the following five categories:

1. Physiological—food, water, sleep.

2. Safety—security of body, relationships, employment, health.

3. Love/belonging—family, friendship, sexual intimacy.

4. Esteem—confidence, achievement, respect.

5. Self-actualization—creativity, knowledge, innovation, achieving one's potential.

According to Maslow's theory, the "lower" order needs beginning with the physiological requirement for food and rest, for example, must be met in order for the individual to progress to "higher" level needs. Without a foundation of safety—the second most important need in Maslow's hierarchy—humans cannot achieve other, higher level needs such as the need for love, connection, creativity, or self-actualization.

Whether you're conscious of it or not, you are continually using your senses to scan people, places, and situations to determine your relative level of safety. The exploratory behavior of animals is a wonderful example of this instinctual and innate habit. With eyes wide open, ears directed toward incoming sound, and heads turning to survey their territory, all animals—including humans—maintain keen vigilance of their surroundings.

While humans and animals share the five basic senses, humans have the added bonus of a sixth sense—intuition. One of the gifts of intuition is that it provides data not necessarily accessible through the five senses. When you're with people who feel safe or in an environment that feels safe, your body and your nervous system relax. If you pay attention to your intuition and your boundaries are healthy and intact, you will instinctively protect yourself when you perceive something, or someone, to be dangerous or unsafe.

What happens when safety is compromised in some way or when boundaries are violated? Boundary ruptures, betrayals of trust, and other threats to safety create a heightened sense of danger and distrust. If you've ever been the victim of a crime, even a nonviolent one, you know that the effects of the incident can linger and impact you long after the initial event. You may change your behavior, routine, or habits. You become hypervigilant and anxious when you find yourself in situations that match or mimic the incident when you were victimized.

If you're a partner of a sex addict in the early stages of discovery and disclosure, you may feel that there is no safe place to turn. Much of what you assumed to be true about your sex addict partner and your relationship has been called into question, or worse, proven to be a lie. The person you thought would always be there for you for better or worse is now the source of profound pain.

If you're like most partners, you've probably combed through bank accounts, email messages, phone records, and years of credit card statements looking for clues and evidence of the sex addict's secret life. You may have hired a private investigator or installed a tracking device on the addict's vehicle or phone without his knowledge. These are all ways in which partners of sex addicts attempt to re-establish a sense of safety.

> Safety is a fundamental human need—and safety
> is created by the effective use of boundaries.

BOUNDARIES ARE EVERYWHERE[2]

By definition, a boundary is a line that marks the limits of an area or a dividing line. In the physical realm, boundaries mark territories and borders. They create defined and contained space, partitions between spaces, and perimeters.

Your experience of your personal boundaries is operating in the background of your awareness almost continuously. As you're reading this book, notice where you are in the space you're in,

---

[2] The information and concepts presented in this chapter regarding basic boundaries, how they operate, and the concept of "offending from the victim position" are adapted from the work of Pia Mellody.

and reflect on the reasons you chose that particular place. Maybe you're sitting in a favorite chair or perhaps you're in a room with the door closed. If you're in a bookstore, you may be sitting in a quiet nook that gives you a sense of comfort and privacy. Your choices about where you're sitting, the direction you're facing, and whether or not the door is closed are all examples of your physical boundaries. Boundaries calm the nervous system, allowing you to relax and rest.

In relationships, boundaries are limits we set with others and ourselves. Setting limits with yourself includes everyday activities such as how much you eat, how many hours you sleep, how many hours you spend working or parenting, or how much time you allow yourself to relax or have fun.

Boundaries, in their most basic form, operate in relationships in the following ways:

Self

- This object, thought, emotion, or behavior belongs to me. I have a right to my possessions, thoughts, emotions, and behaviors (provided they don't violate the boundaries of others). No one has the right to tell me what I may own, think, feel, or do.

- This is as close as I want to be to you—sexually, physically, intellectually, or emotionally—and I have a right to determine the distance.

Others

- This object, thought, emotion, or behavior belongs to you. You have a right to your possessions, thoughts, emotions, and behaviors (provided they don't violate the boundaries of others). No one, including me, has the right to tell you what you may own, think, feel, or do.

- This is as close as you want me to be to you—sexually, physically, intellectually, or emotionally. You have a right to determine the distance, and I accept your limits.

Your personal boundaries serve two primary purposes:

1. They create safety by protecting you from others and protecting others from your boundary-less, inappropriate, or offensive behavior.

2. They define who you are, as well as your personal space, by letting others know how close they can get to you physically, sexually, intellectually, emotionally, or spiritually. Like a physical fence, personal boundaries communicate, "this is me/mine" and "this is you/yours."

When protective boundaries are weak or nonexistent, you are at risk of having your boundaries violated by others. You won't notice danger when you're with people or in situations that aren't safe, or you will feel unsafe in situations that are actually safe. You may feel as though you're being taken advantage of, not getting your needs met, or that your life is chaotic and unmanageable. Because you don't know how to get your needs and wants met directly or assertively, you may unknowingly resort to passive strategies of manipulation and control. If your protective boundary is severely impaired, you won't have confidence and trust in your ability to protect yourself.

COMMON MISCONCEPTIONS AND MYTHS ABOUT BOUNDARIES

The way boundaries work in relationships is often misinterpreted and misunderstood. Boundaries are sometimes seen as harsh, cold, or uncaring. They're also mistakenly viewed as punishment carried out by rigid, uptight, or selfish people. Because boundaries create limits, they're sometimes interpreted as repressive or as restrictions on personal freedom.

A common misconception about boundary work is that a choice to protect yourself—as an act of self-care—is a punishment of the other person. For example, if the sex addict has repeatedly been irresponsible with money and has broken financial agreements, you may decide to get a separate bank account. The choice to get a separate account is not a punishment of him. It's an act of self-care for you and a rational response to repeated boundary violations.

One of the most damaging misconceptions about boundaries is that you don't have a right to protect yourself because of what happened to you in the past. Underneath this misconception is usually an unconscious belief that the person is defective or broken as a result of having his or her boundaries violated as a child or having experienced one, or several, traumatic events as an adult. If you were frequently abused—either verbally, emotionally, physically, or sexually—you may unknowingly carry a deeply held belief that you don't have a right to protect yourself. This is simply not true. No matter what has happened to you or what you have done, you have a right to set limits for yourself around how others treat you.

One of the biggest misconceptions about boundaries is that they give us permission to tell someone else what to do or not do. In a parent-child relationship, a parent can tell the child what he or she can or cannot do. However, in adult-adult relationships, you can make a request for a change of behavior, but you can't demand any action or behavior from another person.

Sometimes partners say, "I told him my boundary is that he has to go to therapy every week." Of course, it may be appropriate and even necessary for the sex addict to go to therapy once a week. You can *request* that the sex addict engage in a particular activity or behavior, but he has a right to say yes, to say no, or to negotiate an alternative agreement. You have the power to create a boundary about what *you* will do if your partner says no to your request that he go to therapy, but you cannot create a boundary that requires another adult to do, act, or behave in a certain way. Chapter Seven covers, in detail, how to make effective requests in boundary work. In the meantime, it's important to understand this crucial concept about how boundaries work.

> Boundaries aren't something you do to another person. Boundaries are something you do for your own self-care, well-being, and protection.

THE FIVE BOUNDARIES

As a partner of a sex addict, you must understand the basics of boundaries so you can determine where you're uncomfortable, vulnerable, or at risk. The four primary boundaries are:

1. Physical

2. Sexual

3. Listening

4. Talking

There is also a fifth type of boundary—the personal energy boundary—which is an intuitive or "felt sense" of another person.

Physical Boundaries

Physical boundaries are about how close you allow others to get to you physically, and the access you give others to your personal property. When physical boundaries are functional, you have the ability to choose how close you get to others physically and how much access you give to your personal property. You are also respectful of others' physical boundaries and respect their right to limit access to their personal property.

Physical boundaries are non-negotiable *personal* boundaries (in contrast to non-negotiable *relationship* boundaries—which are covered later in this chapter). A non-negotiable personal boundary means that when someone says "no" to physical touch or access to his or her personal property, the boundary must be accepted without question or attempts to convince the other person to change his or her mind.

Sexual Boundaries

When your sexual boundaries are functional and intact, you know how to express your sexual needs and wants, as well as how to set limits with your partner about sexual activity that isn't comfortable for you. Sexual boundaries involve the ability to choose with whom, when, where, and how you will be sexual. Sexual boundaries, like physical boundaries, are non-negotiable—meaning a "no" to sexual touch means "no." If your partner says he or she doesn't want sexual touch, or he or she doesn't want touch in a certain way, in a certain area of his or her body, or doesn't want to be sexual in a certain place or location, that boundary is non-negotiable.

If you would like sexual touch or activity in a particular way, but your partner isn't open to it, you should talk to your partner about it and discuss why it's important to you. Your partner may change her or his mind after hearing why it's important to you. However, no one's sexual limits should be altered as a result of coercion or threat.

In the past, you may have believed you had to do what the sex addict asked you to do sexually. Sadly, many religious communities teach couples that husbands have a right to their wives' bodies at all times. This is physical, sexual, and spiritual/religious abuse.

You may have been told that you were rigid or a prude because you weren't comfortable with watching pornography or other sexual practices. Most partners have engaged in sexual activity with which they're uncomfortable. Many have been sexually harassed and abused by the sex addict. If this is the case for you, I urge you to find ways to express your pain and anger, and to release any shame about what happened to you or what you may have gone along with in the past. Pay attention to your discomfort—it's giving you crucial information about your sexual preferences, limits, and boundaries.

Listening Boundary

Listening is the most difficult of the four primary boundaries. The listening boundary is about taking in what you hear and deciding what you think and how you feel about what you've heard. When the listening boundary is functional, you will know how to sort through what you hear and how to protect yourself from taking in other's emotions or any data that isn't true for you. You will also know how to maintain an attitude of curiosity, and how to take a relational time-out when you become flooded emotionally. When the listening boundary is weak, you are vulnerable to painful feelings as a result of misinterpreting what you hear, or taking in others' reality when it doesn't match your own.

Talking Boundary

The talking boundary involves the ability to share your thoughts and emotions in an honest, authentic, and relational manner. When the talking boundary is functional, you have an active filter between what you're thinking and what you say, you regulate your emotions as you speak, and you use appropriate volume and tone. You are also mindful of maintaining a balance between sharing too much or too little, and of time spent talking versus time spent listening.

PARTNERS SPEAK

"Boundaries enhanced communication and decreased the craziness around all the drama and reactivity. They allowed me to take deep breaths and then respond from a loving, feeling place."

—Kay

The Personal Energy Boundary

In addition to the four primary boundaries, there is a fifth category I call the "personal energy boundary." Personal energy is not necessarily something you can hear or see, but is rather an intuitive or "felt sense" of a person that extends or radiates beyond the physical body.

When a person seems to fill up the room so that he or she dominates or unduly draws attention to himself or herself, this is an experience of personal energy. This can happen due to the tone or volume of his or her speech, the way he or she dresses, or behaves. Although he or she is not violating any physical or sexual boundaries, his or her presence may leave little or no space for others to be seen or express themselves. Excessively dramatic or histrionic individuals are examples of this end of the continuum. On the other hand, the personal energy of a depressed or severely shy or timid person may be barely perceived or felt—as if he or she could disappear.

Another example of sensing someone's personal energy is when you're with a person or in a group of people and you experience emotions that seem to come from nowhere or that aren't congruent or consistent with your own mood or internal state in the moment. When this happens, you may be sensing other people's thoughts and/or emotions—their personal energy. If your intuition is particularly strong, you will notice others' energy more keenly and with more regularity.

As a partner, you may sense the sex addict's energy and feel overwhelmed, confused, or crazy without any objective data to support your feelings. You may experience this with other people as well, including strangers. If you do, you can visualize a protective barrier between you and the other person, such as a steel wall, a glass bell, a protective being such as an angel, or another comforting or supportive presence beside you. You can also visualize placing a protective wall around the other person to protect you from his or her energy. If you activate this kind of boundary visualization and your emotions or internal state begins to shift, chances are you were sensing the other person's energy, thoughts, and/or emotions rather than your own.

BOUNDARIES AT THE EXTREMES

To understand how healthy boundaries work, it's important to have an idea of what they look like when they're not in balance—or operating at the extremes.

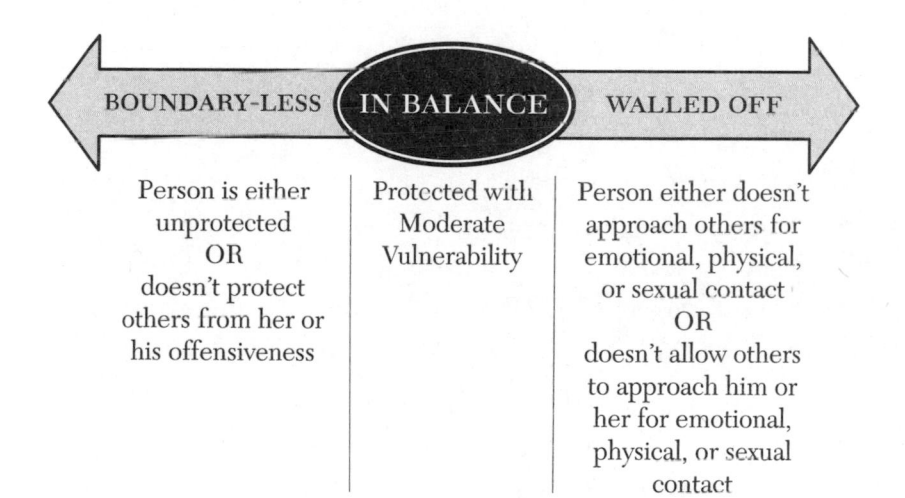

Figure 1. Boundaries at the Extremes

At one extreme, the person is boundary-less, meaning they lack boundaries. Since boundaries are about protection—either protecting us from others or protecting others from our own offensive behavior—being boundary-less can mean one of two things: the person is either unprotected (too vulnerable) or failing to protect others from his or her own offensive behavior.

If you're unprotected or too vulnerable, you allow others to touch you even when you don't want to be touched physically or sexually. You may allow others to cross various lines with you even when you want to say "no." A person who is too vulnerable will have difficulty hearing what others say without taking it personally, or will take on the other person's reality or opinions even when those opinions or beliefs don't match his or her own. These are examples of a person being too vulnerable with regard to the listening boundary.

The boundary-less person who is not protecting others from his or her own offensive behavior may touch others without permission (or even after someone has said "no" to physical/sexual touch), share too much personal information, tell inappropriate jokes, or give unsolicited advice. When someone is boundary-less around protecting others, we sometimes say they lack containment.

On the other end of the continuum, the person is walled off or invulnerable. To be walled off or invulnerable means you don't allow others to get close to you—emotionally, intellectually, physically, or sexually. In terms of interpersonal communication, a walled off person won't take in what others say and won't share with others what he or she is thinking, feeling, or what's important to him or her. They are essentially positioned "behind a wall"— emotionally, intellectually, physically, sexually, and relationally.

Most people operate somewhere between the extremes of boundary-lessness and being walled off; however, you will tend to gravitate toward one end of the continuum or the other with regard to each of the four primary boundaries. Keep in mind that it's possible to be boundary-less in one area and walled off in another. For example, you may allow others to touch you or your personal belongings even when you don't want them to (boundary-less/unprotected), while at the same time never asking or seeking physical touch from others (walled off). If you'd like to know where you stand with each of the primary boundaries, see the Boundary Evaluation in the Appendix.

Ideally, the goal is to seek balance by hovering somewhere around midline between being boundary-less and walled off. This is the state of being protected with moderate vulnerability. When considering what it means to be in balance, I like to use the analogy of holding a balancing pose in yoga. When you're standing on one foot, you're never perfectly still. As you maintain your balance, you sway and wobble—even slightly—from side to side. The same is true with the practice of personal and relationship boundaries. The idea is not to reach perfection, but to avoid the extremes and stay close to the midline.

PARTNERS SPEAK

"During the most toxic years of our relationship, I held the belief that boundaries were obstacles I set around his behaviors to control him. After years of recovery, I have come to understand and know that the boundaries I set around his behaviors are the tools I use in order for me to feel safe and protected. The boundaries I set around my own behaviors are the tools I use to gift him with the opportunity to trust and feel safe with me."

—Jadine

WHAT ARE BOUNDARY VIOLATIONS?

Boundaries can be broken in a number of ways. Generally speaking, there are two types of boundary intrusions: boundary ruptures and boundary violations.

Boundary ruptures occur when a boundary is violated, but in an impersonal or unintentional way. Injuries from car accidents, natural disasters, or any incident outside the reasonable control of another person are boundary ruptures. There can also be unintentional breaches of personal or private space. For example, having a stranger enter your dressing room in a store as you're changing clothes because the lock on the door didn't close properly is an example of an unintentional boundary rupture. Boundary ruptures, even though they lack malicious intent, can be distressing, painful, and even traumatic.

Boundary violations are any unwanted intrusion of your emotional, physical, or sexual space caused by the boundary-less behavior of another person. Boundary violations don't necessarily imply a malicious intent on the part of another person. For example, many people go to work when they have a fever or other contagious illness. This is a boundary violation because the person is exposing others to his or her illness. However, the person probably doesn't wish or intend for others to get sick. He or she is simply unconscious or in denial about the fact that his or her behavior is boundary-less.

Physical Boundary Violations

The following are examples of physical boundary violations experienced by partners of sex addicts (including those where the partner may violate the sex addict's boundaries).

- Blocking or preventing a person from leaving any private/public space.

- Attempting to limit or prevent someone from having regular contact with family or friends for the purpose of controlling and isolating the person.

- Touching someone without her or his permission (including while sleeping, unconscious, or blacked out).

- Looking through the personal belongings of another person without her or his permission (including computer history, email, or phone records, wallet, purse, etc.).

- Monitoring another person's communications without her or his permission (phone, email, text, or social media).

- Physical abuse of any kind (for example, hitting, grabbing, slapping, hair pulling, pinching, shoving, and so on).

- Exposing others to witnessing physical abuse (for example, physically fighting in the presence of children).

- Throwing or breaking things in the presence of others, which is a form of intimidation and threat.

- Denying others personal or private space (for example, not allowing a person to change clothes, bathe, or groom privately).

There are certain "safety seeking" behaviors in which most partners of sex addicts engage that are boundary violations; for example, looking at the addict's phone or computer records. Although it is highly problematic to condone the practice of violating another person's boundary—as if the person crossing the boundary were "above the law"—it is completely logical and understandable that partners in the early stages of discovery will engage in some of these behaviors.

Many partners describe getting lost in futile, adrenalin-fueled, and often traumatic detective work while they're supposed to be working or caring for young children. When partners spend hours going through credit card statements, checking phone records, or searching online for former acting-out partners or evidence of the sex addict's activities long after discovery or therapeutic disclosure, they are in a powerless and self-destructive cycle that keeps them stuck, re-traumatized, and feeling like a victim.

Over time and with a better understanding of boundaries and self-care, partners will transition from these kinds of safety-seeking behaviors to trusting their instincts—*even in the face of deception.* They will act on their instincts without the need to gather more data to support their choices. Making the shift from safety seeking detective-related behaviors to self-care and boundaries is at the heart of partners' healing and the 5-SBS.

Any discussion of physical boundary violations wouldn't be complete without mentioning that physical abuse—hitting, slapping, choking, etc.—of sex addicts by their partners happens more frequently than you might think. Partners who physically abuse the sex addict rationalize their behavior by saying the addict deserved it. This is the same distorted thinking that causes women around the world to be physically punished, and even stoned to death, for being unfaithful to their husbands. This kind of unrestrained retribution is best described as "offending from the victim position," which is covered in Chapter Six. There is no justification for physically abusing another person—ever.

Sexual Boundary Violations

Partners of sex addicts frequently experience challenges and violations of their sexual boundaries. Here are the most common:

- Being shamed by the sex addict for your sexual preferences or boundaries.

- Saying "no" to sex and being repeatedly prodded, harassed, or even forced to be sexual with the addict. Forced sex of any kind in marriage is marital rape, and is illegal in every state in the United States including the District of Columbia.[3]

---

[3] Rape, Abuse & Incest National Network (RAINN). "Intimate Partner Sexual Violence," www.rainn.org/public-policy/sexual-assault-issues/marital-rape (accessed May 15, 2015).

- Being touched sexually by the addict without your permission (including while sleeping, blacked out, or unconscious).

- Being exposed to a sexually transmitted disease without your knowledge (for example, not being told that your sexual partner has genital herpes or HIV/AIDS).

- Children exposed to age-inappropriate sexual information/behavior due to the addict's behaviors (for example, pornography, sexual conversations, sexual activity between parents, inappropriate nudity).

- Ongoing deception about the addict's sexual activities outside the relationship.

- Addict making frequent or inappropriate references to sex or sexuality in conversation.

- Being led to believe that the addict is using birth control when he or she isn't.

Listening Boundary Violations

Because listening is primarily a boundary of self-protection rather than containment, there are fewer potential boundary violations than with physical, sexual, or talking boundaries. Listening boundary violations include the following:

- Nonverbal communication such as eye rolling.

- Tuning someone out or refusing to listen while they're attempting to be relational or intimate.

Talking Boundary Violations

Because of the dishonesty and deception inherent in relationships affected by sex addiction, most partners have experienced severe and ongoing violations of the talking boundary. Here are some examples of talking boundary violations partners of sex addicts experience:

- Lying, gaslighting, or attempts to obscure reality by the sex addict for the purpose of deception.

- Blaming the partner, especially when attempting to deflect or avoid responsibility.

- Breaking an agreement or commitment without good cause.

- Being told what you think or don't think.

- Being told how you feel or don't feel.

- Name-calling, using sarcasm, or ridiculing.

- Repeatedly and intentionally interrupting.

- Attempting to manipulate or control.

- Raging, yelling, or screaming.

NON-NEGOTIABLE RELATIONSHIP BOUNDARIES

By definition, a non-negotiable boundary is a boundary that is not open to discussion or modification. In terms of the basic personal boundaries discussed, a non-negotiable boundary simply means that "no" means "no"—it is not open to discussion or negotiation. This is especially true for physical and sexual boundaries.

Another type of non-negotiable boundary is a non-negotiable relationship boundary. Non-negotiable relationship boundaries involve *something you must have* or *something you can't tolerate* in order to stay in a relationship. Non-negotiable relationship boundaries are relationship deal-breakers.

As relationship deal-breakers, non-negotiable boundaries must be carefully considered and chosen. In my work with partners, I often find that non-negotiable boundaries are confused with important needs. For example, it's completely understandable that you would have a need for any, or all, of the following from your sex addict partner:

- Regular attendance at twelve-step meetings.

- Ongoing therapy.

- Transparency around use of email accounts and phone records.

- Disclosure polygraph and/or follow-up polygraphs.

However, for most partners these aren't appropriate non-negotiable boundaries. If you're not prepared to leave the relationship if your partner doesn't fulfill one of these needs, the boundary isn't non-negotiable.

When emotions are running high or you're triggered, you'll be tempted to create a list of non-negotiable boundaries that look something like this:

- Addict must go to five twelve-step meetings per week for a specified number of years.

- Addict must meet with sponsor once a week.

- Addict must not have any contact with any former acting-out partner.

- Addict must not have a recovery slip (meaning a violation of his bottom line/inner circle behaviors).

- Addict must take a polygraph every three months for a specified number of years.

- Addict must have a filter on all electronic devices for five years.

While most of these items are beneficial for the addict's recovery and the rehabilitation of your relationship, it's important for you to ask yourself two crucial questions before putting them on your non-negotiable boundaries list:

1. Is each one of these boundaries, individually, a relationship deal-breaker?

2. Am I absolutely unwilling to discuss—negotiate—these items with my partner?

For example, are you prepared to leave the relationship if your partner misses a therapy session? Or misses a meeting with his sponsor? Or asks you after two years of passed polygraphs to reduce the frequency of his exams?

Most likely, you would be disappointed if he didn't follow through on one of the items on the list, but you probably wouldn't leave him because of it. That's why it shouldn't be on your list of non-negotiable boundaries.

Such non-negotiable boundary lists create the following dynamics for you personally and for your relationship:

- Unhealthy and toxic power imbalances in your relationship created by unilateral rules and regulations about issues that aren't ultimately relationship deal-breakers.

- Conflict and power struggles between you and the sex addict as he attempts to comply with your boundary list under threat of losing the relationship.

- Repeated disappointments for you as the addict will inevitably break one of your non-negotiable boundaries.

- You become untrustworthy to yourself and your partner as you struggle to respond to or follow through on consequences for "boundary violations" when your non-negotiable boundaries aren't met.

- Even when it's appropriate or makes sense for your situation, you're unwilling to discuss with the addict how boundaries might be altered or renegotiated—after all, they're non-negotiable!

Most partners have no more than two or three non-negotiable boundaries. Boundaries—especially non-negotiable ones—are specific and unique to you. No one can/should tell you what your boundaries must be. However, to give you some guidance, here are some common non-negotiable boundaries set by partners of sex addicts:

- Causing harm to, or any sexual activity with, a minor.

- Viewing child pornography.

- Sexual intercourse with another person.

- Repeated deception or lying.

When identifying non-negotiable boundaries, ask yourself:

"What would absolutely, positively, without question, cause me to know beyond a shadow of a doubt that I can no longer stay in this relationship?" Your answers are your non-negotiable boundaries.

Knowing your non-negotiable relationship boundaries creates clarity and gives you a sense of your limits. When you've identified your non-negotiable boundaries, share them with a trusted friend, sponsor, or therapist. You can then share them with your sex addict partner—not as a threat—but as an exercise in telling him your reality, your limits, and as an expression of your self-care and self-respect.

WHAT GOOD BOUNDARIES CAN DO FOR YOU

The practice of good boundaries is second only to self-care as an essential survival strategy for partners of sex addicts. In fact, boundaries are one of the clearest expressions of self-care and self-love. When you have the courage to ask yourself, "What do I need and want?" and you take the necessary steps to get those needs and wants met, you are lightyears ahead of most people.

Sadly, many of us wait for others to notice our needs and wants. We may even make indirect or passive attempts to get our needs met, by saying things like, "Boy, wouldn't it be nice to go to that new Italian restaurant?" rather than, "I would love to go to that new Italian restaurant. Would you like to go with me Friday night?" When others don't take the hint or don't read our mind, we feel forgotten, unloved, or like a victim.

It takes courage and vulnerability to ask for what you need and want. After all, the other person may say no. On the other hand, there is a warm, confident, and magnetic presence that radiates from people who are experts at getting their needs and wants met. Make it your mission to become one of those people.

Here is a short list of the great things you can expect from good boundaries:

- A sense of safety, as you learn how to protect yourself and others emotionally, physically, and sexually.

- Clear communication.

- The ability to make important improvements in your life as you set limits on your own behaviors that you want to upgrade or change.

- The ability to define your limits physically, sexually, emotionally, and intellectually, and to communicate those limits in your relationships.

- Knowing where you stand in relationships rather than wondering or guessing.

- Knowing how to determine whether or not a relationship is salvageable.

- The ability to act from authentic personal power versus "power over" others (covered in Chapter Six).

- The ability to define who you are and express your authentic self.

"Boundaries are a source of liberation."

—Greg McKeown, *Essentialism: The Disciplined Pursuit of Less*

COMMON BOUNDARIES SET BY PARTNERS OF SEX ADDICTS

Partners of sex addicts must become experts at boundary work. Without boundaries, your life with the sex addict will be uncertain at best and dangerous at worst. Boundaries, like most things in life, are fluid and ever changing. That means there will be some boundaries you will create in early discovery that you will later relax or completely let go.

One example of a boundary that frequently changes over time is sexual contact. I strongly recommend that partners abstain from unprotected sexual contact with the sex addict until after formal therapeutic disclosure (with polygraph) for the simple reason that you don't have enough information about your partner's sexual history to make an informed choice about being sexual with him.

Abstaining from *all* sexual contact with the addict can be very helpful, and even illuminating to you as a partner. Engaging in or withholding sex in an attempt to prevent the addict from acting out or being triggered is a form of control. Partners often discover during a period of celibacy that they have unknowingly used sex as a way to calm their fears about the sex addict having a slip or relapse.

Following is a list of common boundaries set by partners, divided into the four primary categories of physical, sexual, listening, and talking boundaries.

Physical Boundaries

- Limiting and/or eliminating physical touch with the sex addict for a period of time.

- Therapeutic separation (in-house or separate housing).

- Sleeping in separate bedrooms.

- Limiting time spent together as a couple or family depending on the addict's engagement in his recovery process or other considerations.

- Separating bank accounts/finances.

- Having no contact with anyone with whom the addict has acted out—whether friends, coworkers, or family members.

- Limiting or eliminating contact with family, friends, coworkers, or acquaintances who have participated in the addict's secret life.

Sexual Boundaries

- Completing STI (sexually transmitted infections) testing.

- Requesting that the sex addict be tested for STIs.

- Refraining from sexual contact with the addict until STI testing has been completed and formal therapeutic disclosure (with polygraph) has taken place.

- Ninety days of celibacy/abstinence from all sexual activity with the sex addict.

- Refraining from engaging in sexual activities with the addict that are uncomfortable, triggering, or outside your value system.

- Installing filters on electronic devices to protect children (or yourself) from unwanted exposure to pornography and/or the sex addict's online acting-out behaviors.

- After the crisis and repair stage, requesting couples' "sexual reintegration" work (see Recommended Reading: Couples/ Communication for more information).

Listening Boundaries

- Taking a time-out from conversations with the addict when interactions are experienced as deceptive, crazy making, or manipulative.

- Making conscious choices about protecting yourself from material (print, online, etc.) that is unnecessarily triggering for you.

- Noticing when the addict's words and actions don't match, and being mindful of the discrepancy without ignoring or minimizing it.

- Noticing when you have received too much detail and/or graphic information about the addict's acting-out behavior, and making a conscious decision to protect yourself in the future from harmful details that don't help the healing process or provide any useful information.

Talking Boundaries

- Deciding with whom and how much to share about your situation.

- Being honest with the sex addict about how his behavior has impacted you without being abusive or shaming (for example, yelling, cursing, or name-calling).

• Making requests of the addict for trust-building behaviors. For example, recovery work; installing filtering or monitoring software on electronic devices; transparency regarding his activities and whereabouts; access to financial information, bank, and email accounts; and weekly recovery check-ins with you. Suggested items for a couples' recovery check-in can be found in the Appendix.

As you're beginning to identify and create your boundaries, pay particular attention to the emotion of anger. One of the gifts of anger is that it's often a signal that a boundary of some kind has been crossed or needs to be set. Begin noticing the emotion of anger when it arises and ask whether there may be a need for a boundary of some kind.

A word of caution: Boundary work is not for the faint of heart. Prepare yourself for pushback, backlash, and outright hostility as you begin practicing better self-care in the form of boundary work. Your partner and others may wonder, "What happened to that sweet ____(your name)____ we used to know?" Know that this is a good sign. It means you're doing something different—something healing and affirming for you.

When you begin to practice good boundaries you may be accused of being self-centered, rigid, paranoid, or over the top. If this happens, ask yourself, "Am I violating anyone's boundaries?" If the answer is no, then remind yourself that only you will suffer if you choose to please others rather than please yourself. This is not selfish behavior. When you fiercely guard your right to your own needs and wants rather than depleting yourself with people pleasing, you naturally become more joyful, generous, and easygoing—and that benefits everyone!

Regardless of your history with setting boundaries, boundary work is a skill that can be learned and implemented right away.

Now that you have a solid foundation of the key components of good, healthy boundaries, let's get started with the first step of the 5-SBS. Knowing and owning your reality will help you begin the process of repairing the damage done by the deception, gaslighting, and crazy making that goes hand in hand with addiction.

CHAPTER FOUR

Boundary Solution Step 1: Knowing and Owning Your Reality

PARTNERS SPEAK

"I really didn't know about boundaries until recovery. Setting boundaries and making healthy choices based on my reality, my truth, and my connection to my Higher Power are huge gifts I received from recovery."

—Paula R.

WHY YOU'VE STRUGGLED TO KNOW YOUR REALITY

If you've been in a relationship with an addict for any length of time, your trust in your own reality and intuition is damaged. Addicts will risk almost anything for their addiction including their livelihood, friends, extended family, primary intimate relationship, their relationship with their children, and even their life. Given the power of addiction, it's no surprise that addicts go to great lengths to hide their behaviors and their secret life.

Sex addicts in particular often avoid talking about anything that could possibly lead to a conversation about sex or their own sexuality in an attempt to protect the addiction. In their primary relationship, addicts may have little or no interest in having sex with their partner or may appear sexually anorexic. If this is the case in your relationship, you will be even less likely to suspect your partner is acting out sexually. Over time, the addict's deception and double life erodes your trust in your reality and intuition.

I often hear partners berate themselves by saying, "How could I have not known?" or "I was so stupid to have believed his lies." If you fall into the trap of blaming yourself for being deceived, remember that the sex addict in your life has made conscious efforts to confuse, omit, or otherwise obscure the truth.

No one wants to believe that one's partner would be unfaithful or intentionally deceptive. When you got close to finding out about his secret life, he probably distracted, cajoled, lied, or maybe even abused you. When this happens, partners often attempt to incorporate the addict's lies into their own reality and wind up feeling confused, foolish, or crazy. Living with active and ongoing deception may have caused you to doubt almost everything you believed you knew or experienced in the relationship prior to discovery.

In early discovery, partners of sex addicts experience a profound and lasting shift in the way they view themselves, their relationship, and even the world. What you understood your reality to be pre-discovery has been shattered. In an attempt to make sense of the new and devastating information you've received, you will likely begin to view most—if not all—of your experiences through the lens of sex addiction, deceit, and betrayal. This is a natural and normal response to your situation and an attempt to create some semblance of order and safety.

Every billboard, sexually oriented business, attractive person, "men's" magazine, and countless other triggers feel like daggers re-injuring an open wound. You will have many questions and worries that come up, even in ordinary daily activities and encounters. Because you don't yet have all the information about the addict's behaviors and history, there will be no limit to the questions and concerns you have about him. After all, pre-discovery you never would have thought he could have done the things you now know he did. Thankfully, this period of time where you feel assaulted by so many external triggers doesn't last forever. But it's painful nonetheless.

Once your reality has been damaged by deception, and then altered by seeing the world through the sex addiction lens, you may fall into the trap of believing that you can gain a better understanding of the way the sex addict thinks and behaves by trying to view other people and situations through his eyes. It's understandable to seek a sense of safety or control by understanding the way the addict thinks. However, attempting to see the world through his eyes is ultimately painful, misguided, and more to the point—impossible. Addictive thinking is fundamentally distorted, contradictory, and illogical.

As tempting as it is to want to "get inside the addict's head," you will gain clarity, safety, and serenity by rebuilding trust in your own perceptions rather than focusing on the addict or trying to see the world as he sees it. Luckily, you *can* restore trust in your own reality and intuition beginning now.

HOW DECEPTION CREATES TRAUMA AND DISTORTS YOUR REALITY

There has been a shift in perspective over the past five to ten years about how partners of sex addicts are perceived and treated by psychotherapists and others in the field of sex addiction treatment. In the early days, otherwise caring and skilled therapists often perceived partners as overly reactive or dramatic. They were sometimes referred to as "borderline," suggesting they had Borderline Personality Disorder. What many therapists failed to understand was the impact of the sex addict's ongoing manipulation, gaslighting, deception, and abuse on their partners.

Discovering that you're in a relationship with a sex addict involves confronting a deep, personal betrayal. It is one thing for your partner to choose to drink or gamble to the point of self-destruction or financial ruin, but it is quite another when your partner chooses sex with himself or others over sex with you. The consequences of being in relationship with an alcohol or other drug addict or gambler can be severe. However, the wound of chronic sexual betrayal can impact you in a more profound and intimate way—emotionally, physically, and sexually.

The sex addict often tells himself that his sexual behaviors and activities outside the relationship have nothing to do with his partner. Regardless of the addict's perception and experience, partners invariably feel rejected, less than, and "second best" as a result of the addict's behaviors. They ask themselves, "What is wrong with me?" or "Why did he choose her/him (or pornography) over me?"

Added to the painful rejection partners feel is the deceit and gaslighting that has permeated the relationship. You may wonder how you could have missed the clues. You may feel stupid or duped, as if you should have been able to see clearly through the dense fog that is active addiction. If you've been labeled a co-addict or co-sex addict, the label may reinforce your fear that you're at fault for the addiction or that you somehow played a role in it.

If you have been repeatedly deceived and lied to, you begin to feel crazy as if you can't trust your own judgments, perceptions, and inner knowing. You may repeatedly wonder whether the sex addict is right and you're wrong. You may often question yourself because what seems obvious to you is labeled as inaccurate, paranoid, or irrational. Sadly, these are common experiences for partners. The sexual and emotional betrayal, along with ongoing deception, traumatizes partners and impairs their ability to trust themselves.

PARTNERS SPEAK

"After his second failed polygraph I really started to wonder if he was one of those people they talk about in the AA Big Book who are constitutionally incapable of telling the truth. I was so confused. I didn't know what to believe. Part of me thought that underneath all the secretiveness and the addiction he was really a good man. But there was another part of me that felt crazy from all the lies, omissions, and half-truths. My imagination went wild thinking of all the things he could have done. It got so bad that at one point I even wondered if he was a sociopath. That was the worst time for me. That period between finding out I was married to a sex addict and when I started to rely more on my own intuition rather than believing that he would tell me what was real."

—Lynn T.

In addition to the emotional abuse of ongoing deception and psychological manipulation, many partners endure covert and sometimes overt physical or sexual abuse as discussed in Chapter Three. These are boundary violations and must be treated as such (tools for addressing boundary violations are discussed in Chapter Eight).

Most partners experience at least two to three symptoms of Post-Traumatic Stress Disorder (PTSD), including the following:

• Severe anxious episodes or panic attacks. These are most common in the pre-discovery or pre-disclosure stage.

- Flashbacks, intrusive thoughts or images that originate from information the addict has shared, from images found inadvertently, or while searching the addict's computer history or email account.

- Nightmares.

- Loss of a sense of safety—physical, emotional, and sexual. Partners experience frequent and sometimes intense triggers from everyday sexual content in conversations, media, etc. They may go through a period of perceiving most men as sex addicts.

- Disillusionment or loss of hope about men/women, the relationship, or their future.

- Numbing or "checking out" to avoid painful feelings through compulsive eating, excessive playing of electronic games, compulsive working, shopping, exercising, etc.

- Disturbances of sleep and eating patterns.

- Inability to focus.

- Preoccupation, obsessive thoughts, or rumination about the addict's activities (past and present), affair partners, or the future in general.

Some partners meet the criteria for a PTSD diagnosis, depending on the level of deception and manipulation they have experienced, along with other factors such as their pre-relationship trauma history. If you have experienced many of these symptoms, you may need specialized trauma treatment such as Somatic Experiencing (SE) or Eye Movement Desensitization and Reprocessing (EMDR). Even for partners who don't have a PTSD diagnosis, these specialized trauma treatments can be beneficial for improving or resolving distressing symptoms.

Fortunately, it is possible to regain trust in your perceptions and intuition. Repairing the damage done by ongoing deception, manipulation, and abuse is a process that begins with the simple yet powerful practice of identifying your reality.

HOW TO IDENTIFY YOUR REALITY IN THREE STEPS

Most of us don't know how to identify our reality. What typically happens is that we have an experience of some kind and then we respond--or react—according to our habits or our conditioned way of perceiving events and other people. We don't stop to think critically about what just happened or analyze it in a systematic way. Basically, we experience something, make up a story about it, and then proceed to act according to the story we made up about it, rather than what may have actually happened.

For example, you pass a coworker in the hall at the office and she doesn't look at you or respond to your "hello." Based on that experience, you think she's angry with you because of something that happened yesterday. You then avoid her for the rest of the day because you're afraid of her reaction. Or, you follow her to her desk and ask, "Why are you angry with me?" The reality is that she just got some bad news or she just realized she missed a deadline, was distracted, or didn't even see you passing her in the hall. This is an example of how we regularly create a distorted reality without realizing it. Your reality in this moment is based on three facts: what you're experiencing, what you think about what you're experiencing, and the emotions you're feeling.

The following three questions will help you identify your reality:

1. What happened? What did I experience with my five senses—eyes, ears, nose, taste, and touch?

2. What do I think? What are my perceptions about what I experienced?

3. What do I feel? What are my emotional responses to what I experienced and perceived?

The first step is to identify the data you heard, saw, or experienced. Data must be something you could record with a video camera. An example of data is: "When I asked my partner why he was late coming home, he said I was harassing him."

Data is often confused with perception and judgment, so that the statement above comes out sounding something like, "My partner was mean and defensive when he came home and I asked him why he was late." Note that words like "mean" and "defensive" are perceptions or judgments rather than objective data. You may perceive that what the other person did was mean or defensive, but in this first step you're identifying the data only. When you get to the second question you can add your thoughts about the data.

The second step is to identify what you think about the data. Here you get to state your perception. Regarding the data above, you might say: "What I thought about it was that he doesn't care about my feelings," or "He was defensive," or "He must have had a bad day." When stating thoughts the phrase "what I made up about that" is sometimes suggested to remind us that our thoughts are not the truth with a capital "T," but rather our personal truth. Saying, "what I made up about that," indicates that we understand that what is true for us may not be true for the other person.

Notice that the first thought, "What I thought was that he doesn't care about my feelings," is a personal interpretation of the incident, whereas the second two thoughts are about the person who is being observed. This is an important distinction, as you will see when we get to the third and last step of identifying your reality.

When working with thoughts, keep in mind there are many possible thoughts that can originate from the same data. Most people have a habit of interpreting events with the same thought. For example, you may often interpret the meaning of interactions and events through a lens that tells you that you're not good enough, or that you're not likeable, or that you have chronically bad luck. These automatic thoughts usually come from beliefs or stories you carry about yourself that are deep-rooted and unconscious.

If you notice you regularly have the same interpretation or thoughts about the events in your life, try generating at least two or three alternative explanations for what happened. This exercise of generating alternative explanations will help increase your awareness that there are a multitude of different perspectives and possibilities about the data you've experienced.

Another helpful thought exercise I recommend is called the "least pathological explanation." While you may not want to use this regularly with an addict who is still active in his addiction, it's a helpful tool nonetheless. There is something about the human mind that leads it to interpret events in their most negative light, especially as it reflects on other people and ourselves. One of the ways to give someone the benefit of the doubt until you get more information is to find the least pathological explanation. For the example above about the coworker not speaking to you, the least pathological explanation might be, "she must not have seen me." Generating a least pathological explanation is also a useful tool to avoid worry, obsession, and other unhelpful thought habits.

The third step is identifying the emotions you experience as a result of the thoughts you're thinking. The eight basic emotions are:

1. Anger
2. Love
3. Guilt
4. Fear
5. Passion
6. Joy
7. Pain
8. Shame

Emotions and their "felt sense" in the body are particularly helpful to partners. When it comes to boundaries and boundary work, anger is a helpful and instructive emotion that functions as a signal that there is a need to create a boundary of some kind—

either with ourselves or with others. Women often struggle with feeling and expressing anger because of negative stereotypes that portray angry women as difficult or as acting like "bitches." Women are further challenged around owning their anger due to often being in the role of caretaker or otherwise being pressured to be a "nice girl" and to not rock the boat.

> *"Anger can be a wonderful wake up call to help you understand what you need and what you value."*
>
> —Marshall Rosenberg

Emotions are mental states that are accompanied by physical sensations. You may have a physiological response to an event without knowing exactly why. For example, when you feel fear, your hands may get sweaty, your voice may become shaky, or your heart rate may increase. When you feel love you may feel physically relaxed or even have a warm sensation in your heart. These physical sensations and the emotions that go with them are information about how you're experiencing situations or people in your environment. It's helpful to notice these physical signs even when you aren't sure where they came from or don't have thoughts to help you make sense of them. As you become more attuned to physical sensations you will begin to notice the emotions that go along with them.

Once you master this system of identifying your reality, you will find that the emotions you feel are a result of your thoughts and perceptions rather than the data. This comes as a surprise to most people because we tend to think our emotions are based on the data rather than on our thoughts.

Why are our emotions a result of our thoughts? If you consider the three thoughts mentioned earlier regarding the addict who became defensive when his partner asked him why he was late, you will notice that the emotions you feel depend on which of the three thoughts you have. For the first thought—"He doesn't care about my feelings"—the emotion may be pain. For the second thought—"He was defensive"—the emotion may be anger. For the third thought—"He must have had a bad day"—the emotion may be compassion or even love. Isn't it remarkable to see the difference in our responses depending on how we choose to interpret a situation? That's why it's so important to know and be conscious of your thoughts about the data you experience.

In intimate relationships we have a tendency to perceive what the other person does or says as personal. In other words, we interpret their behavior as being "about us" in some way. Most people's behavior is solely about them and who they are. If your thought about why the sex addict betrayed you is, "I wasn't attractive enough," or "I didn't have sex with him often enough," you will have different emotions than if your thought is, "He has an addiction."

By no means am I suggesting that you should not feel pain, anger, or sadness about the sex addict's behavior. You have a right to all those emotions. The addict's behavior absolutely impacts you, but it is not about you. As the Al-Anon slogan says, "You didn't cause it, you can't control it, and you can't cure it." Understanding that you're not at fault, not to blame, and not less valuable than acting-out partners or porn stars can make a huge difference in how you navigate through your healing process.

Emotions must be acknowledged, rather than ignored, repressed, or unexpressed. They also must be "owned." That means when you realize you're angry you not only acknowledge the emotion of anger but you're also willing and ready to take action, if needed, to express your anger or to protect yourself from a similar situation arising in the future. When you don't own your emotions you become stuck and put yourself in situations where you experience the same scenarios over and over. Your life becomes a kind of "Groundhog Day" where you repeat patterns with yourself or with others that leave you feeling angry, hurt, or disempowered. If this is true for you, the problem is not with the people or the situations, but with your struggle around taking necessary actions based on prior painful experiences. The 5-SBS will help you take action so that you can avoid feeling repeatedly injured or even traumatized.

Once you put these three pieces together—data, thought, and emotion—you will be able to create reality statements like the following:

"When I asked my partner why he was late coming home and he said I was harassing him, what I thought about that (or what I made up about that) is that he didn't care about my feelings. And about that I feel pain, fear, and anger."

Or

"When I asked my partner why he was late coming home and he said I was harassing him, what I thought about that (or what I made up about that) is that he was being defensive. And about that I feel fear and anger."

Or

"When I asked my partner why he was late coming home and he said I was harassing him, what I thought about that (or what I made up about that) is that he had a bad day. And about that I feel love and pain."

This three-step exercise will help you identify your own reality and become grounded in it. Knowing and owning your reality is the first step in the process of creating and maintaining your boundaries. Simple as it may appear, it is one of the most effective tools you can use to learn how to think about what is happening to you in any given moment. It can also be used as a template to formulate how to communicate effectively and relationally with another person.

We discuss the use of Pia Mellody's Talking Format for resolving boundary violations in Chapter Eight. For now, we're using the three simple questions on the previous page as a tool for you to rebuild trust and confidence in your perceptions, reality, and intuition.

You may want to keep a notebook or journal with you to make notes about what you're experiencing, especially when you're feeling unsure or foggy, or when the situation feels crazy making in some way. Often when you're feeling "crazy" or foggy, it's another person's behavior, distorted thinking, or covert (hidden) manipulation that is having a negative impact on you. It's in moments like these that you can gain clarity by focusing on your own experience, thoughts, and emotions.

WHAT ABOUT INTUITION?

Partners often have gut feelings or an intuitive sense that something is wrong or that the sex addict is lying or acting out. Intuitive hunches are information that may or may not have concrete data to back it up. They are sometimes experienced as spiritual guidance, or information received from one's Higher Power. While hunches don't neatly fit into the category of data described above—*something you could record with a video camera*—intuition is an important source of information.

In the pre-discovery and early discovery period you may have many intuitive feelings about what the sex addict is doing or you may sense that there is information being withheld from you. This is natural, normal, and accurate. Partners frequently discover after either formal or informal disclosure that many of their intuitive hunches were correct. Addicts often say that their partners have keen intuition, and that is usually true.

However, when you're being deceived and gaslighted, you may have intuitive hunches that later turn out to be inaccurate. This doesn't mean your intuition is wrong. It just means that your intuition is working overtime to compensate for the fact that you're being actively deceived and aren't getting the information you need and deserve.

The combination of your intuitive feelings and the sex addict's gaslighting can be a source of intense anxiety, panic episodes, or feeling crazy. That's because your inner perceptions and the external data don't match. This is enough to make anyone feel disoriented. Don't let the fact that your perceptions have been manipulated by ongoing deceit cause you to lose faith in your intuition. As you become more grounded in your own reality and perceptions, you will start questioning the situation—rather than yourself—when it doesn't feel quite right or make sense to you.

When you have an intuition or a gut feeling about anything, whether it concerns the sex addict or not, trust that your intuition is correct until you receive information that contradicts the intuitive hunch, or something else happens that warrants you changing your mind. For example, if the sex addict tells you that he has only acted out with pornography and hasn't acted out sexually with other people, and your intuition tells you that that is not true, you should protect yourself as if you knew your intuition was, in fact, correct. If you don't act on your intuition in this way, you aren't honoring your reality and you may put yourself at risk unnecessarily. If you discover at a later time that your intuition was inaccurate, you can adjust your behavior accordingly, with the satisfaction of knowing that you trusted your inner knowing and took care of yourself.

One of the great paradoxes of healing from betrayal is that, over time, you focus less on trying to discern whether or not the addict is honest or trustworthy. Instead, you will rely more on your own perceptions and intuition as the primary source of information and safety in your relationship.

"Reality is easy. It's deception that's the hard work."

—Lauryn Hill

A word of caution about the use of intuition: Some partners use intuition as a reason—or justification—to obsessively and excessively monitor, investigate, and even physically follow the sex addict under the guise of validating their reality. While it can be helpful to get data to confirm your intuition, if you find that you're spending inordinate amounts of time collecting information, looking for evidence, or attempting to "catch" the addict in a lie, you are being controlled by the addiction rather than honoring and acting on your own inner knowing.

One of the signs that you are caught in this self-destructive cycle of compulsive data seeking is when you have collected a substantial amount of evidence about the addict's problematic behaviors yet haven't taken meaningful and sustained action toward your self-care or setting boundaries. If this is the case for you, it's time to use the information you already have, own your anger and pain, and move forward with boundary work. Doing anything else keeps you stuck in the victim role.

REALITY CHECKING

In early discovery and disclosure, relying on the sex addict to validate or affirm your reality is risky at best, and disastrous at worst. The qualities of transparency, honesty, and empathy take time to develop in most addicts. That's why you must have other trusted sources to support you in regaining trust in your perceptions and intuition.

Reality checking is a tool you can use when you have a perception but you're struggling to fully own your reality or trust your intuition. For example, you may have had a conversation with the addict that left you feeling confused or unsure. You have one perception about what happened, and he has another. Or the addict said one thing, but his behavior didn't match his words.

When this happens, a partner often attempts to get the addict to understand or validate her reality. Or worse, she ignores her perceptions and adjusts her thinking so she agrees with the addict's perception. When there is a mismatch between your inner knowing and the information you're getting from the sex addict, you can seek out trusted people in your support circle such as friends, therapy group members, sponsors, or therapists to check your reality.

Tell them what happened, using the reality exercise in this chapter, and ask them what they think about it. Having others to connect with in this way is one of the benefits of joining support groups and other communities for partners focused on surviving and healing from betrayal. Communities of support are invaluable for partners of sex addicts. When you bring incidents and issues to other people who have experienced what you're going through and want the best for you, you get support to honor your reality. You may also get a different perspective that helps you see something you may have missed. (For a list of communities for partners of sex addicts see the Appendix.)

Getting clear and grounded about your reality is the first crucial step in beginning the process of restoring safety and trust. It is also the first step of effective boundary work. Take some time now to complete Boundary Solution Step 1.

▇ EXERCISE

BOUNDARY SOLUTION STEP 1: IDENTIFY YOUR REALITY[4]

In order to establish a boundary, you must know your reality or what is true for you. Your reality in the present moment is what you're experiencing with your five senses (sight, sound,

---

[4] Adapted from the work of Pia Mellody.

smell, taste, and physical sensations), what you are thinking, and your emotions. This step may be used for any event, issue, or situation that is causing distress for you—in other words, anything around which you would like to establish a boundary.

Identify your reality by asking yourself three simple questions, and writing down your answers in the "5-SBS Clarifier" (available for download at www.vickitidwellpalmer. com/5sbsclarifier):

1. *Data:* What did I see/hear/experience that could be recorded with a video camera? Write only what you could actually see, hear, or experience with your five senses and don't include perceptions or judgments such as mean, rude, ignored, or harassed. (If your only data is an intuitive hunch, you can describe the intuitive thought or perception as a form of data.)

2. *Thought:* What is my perception/thought, or what do I "make up" about the data? While you may have many thoughts about the data, identify one key thought that has the most energy for you and write it down.

3. *Emotion:* What emotions do I feel as a result of the thought I have about the data? Identify all that apply: anger, pain, guilt, shame, love, fear, passion, joy, etc.

CHAPTER FIVE

Boundary Solution Step 2: Getting Your Needs Met

"In our culture, most of us have been trained to ignore our own wants and to discount our needs."

—*Marshall Rosenberg*

By definition, needs represent a quality or a condition that is necessary or required. Needs are the foundation for building and creating better health (physical, emotional, and spiritual) and better relationships. If you aren't aware of your needs and whether they're being met, you will not be able to create a solution or a boundary that meets that need.

When a situation or relationship is creating discomfort or pain, there is likely a need or perhaps several needs that aren't being met. You may have been taught to ignore or discount your needs, either in your family growing up or in your adult relationships. This can happen in a variety of ways, either overt (obvious) or covert (hidden).

KNOWING YOUR NEEDS

Now that you've completed Boundary Solution Step 1 and are clear about your reality—what's happening, what you think about it, and your emotions—it's time to dig deeper into the specifics of why the current situation isn't workable for you and what you'd like to see in your life or in your relationship going forward. Often, when we're unhappy or in distress, we don't take the time to ask ourselves what we need or want, other than to make the pain stop.

As we discussed in Chapter Three, psychologist Abraham Maslow created a theory of human needs called the *Hierarchy of Needs*. According to Maslow, the most basic human needs are physiological (food, shelter, and sleep, for example), whereas the highest level of human needs are for self-actualization or the realization of our greatest potential.

In between the basic physiological needs and self-actualization are the following:

• Safety

• Connection/Belonging

• Respect

(For a detailed list of needs, see the Needs Inventory in the Appendix.) Other important needs include the need for honesty, peace, and autonomy (independence). Maslow theorized that until the basic or lower order needs are met, the higher order needs can't be attended to. Now, notice how many of these needs are either in serious jeopardy or are outright casualties in relationships where active addiction and deception are present. For example, safety, honesty, and connection are required needs in all intimate relationships. If these foundational needs aren't met, the chances of the relationship surviving, much less thriving, are remote.

In getting needs met, there are some you have the ability to take care of yourself and others you don't. For example, the need for another person to be honest with you is an important need, but one that you can't meet yourself. You can create boundaries to protect yourself from the dishonesty of others or the consequences of others' dishonesty, but you can't influence or cause someone to be honest with you.

When working with needs, you can take action immediately by taking care of the needs over which you have control. This is an important point that can't be emphasized enough. *You must begin to recognize where you have power over an outcome and where you don't.* Partners often spend inordinate amounts of energy and time attempting to get the addict to change. As understandable as it is to want the addict to stop acting out or lying, it's impossible to make it happen. The only person we have control over is us—and sometimes we don't even have control over that! I discuss in greater detail how to identify where you have power, versus where you don't, in Chapter Six.

If your partner has acted out sexually with other people and has potentially exposed you to a sexually transmitted infection or disease, you have a need for physical and sexual safety that's not being met. In this case, meeting the need for safety is well within your power. You can stop sexual contact with the sex addict and you can get tested for sexually transmitted diseases.

Partners sometimes say, "He's the one that had unprotected sex. He should have to get tested, not me." It's true that he's responsible for his behavior and his health, but no one except you is responsible for your health and well-being. The reality is that you don't *have to* get tested. You can choose not to get tested. However, the choice not to get tested has consequences ranging from living with the uncertainty of knowing your health status, to having an untreated and potentially life-threatening illness. It is fundamentally unsafe and simply illogical for you to rely on another person to verify and take care of your physical health.

The healthier, more empowered approach is to ask yourself what you can do to take care of your need for physical health, protect yourself, and take the necessary action. Ideally, you will get tested for STIs, but you could also temporarily stop having sexual contact with your partner or practice safe sex if you choose to be sexual.

When faced with difficult choices like these, it's easy to fall into a victim mindset that tells you that you have to do something because of a poor choice or mistake on the part of another person. This is a dangerous and self-defeating belief that will keep you stuck, angry, and resentful.

I encourage you to get support and feedback about your list of needs and how they can be met. In crises, it's easy to get tunnel vision and struggle to come up with a list of options from which to choose. By identifying your needs, generating possible solutions, and taking action, you will begin to experience more empowerment, clarity, and serenity.

PARTNERS SPEAK

"Prior to recovery, I was numb and totally unaware of my needs/wants. As I began to thaw out and become aware of myself, I became more centered and understood at a cellular level that my happiness is up to me and that I am not in control of my addict's happiness or unhappiness. I now ask myself, 'What is the next right loving step for me?' and listen to my Higher Power's answer."

—Kay

THE "HONESTY PROBLEM" IN EARLY RECOVERY FROM SEX ADDICTION

Working with partners over the years, I've found that the greatest need they have is for honesty. As difficult as it is for sex addicts to believe, most partners can deal with almost any sexual acting-out behavior but they can't tolerate dishonesty. As a partner, you know in your heart that this is a deep truth. Honesty is the foundation of all intimate relationships, yet it's invariably a casualty in relationships where addiction is present. How do you, as a partner, get this fundamental need met during the addict's unpredictable and often turbulent transition from secrecy and deception to transparency and honesty?

The first step is to discover what you need in order to rebuild trust in the addict's word. This step usually includes a variety of actions that demonstrate transparency and accountability on the addict's part. In the beginning, you will need to rely more on your own perceptions and reality and less on the addict's words and promises. However, you can start noticing right now whether his words and actions match. Saying one thing and doing another damages the trust rebuilding process.

TOLERATING THE INTOLERABLE

When it comes to addressing the needs of partners of sex addicts, it's important to acknowledge that there is a period of time in early discovery when basic relationship needs such as trust and honesty are simply nonexistent. Although these are fundamental to any intimate relationship, the reality is that partners must endure a period of time where they simply don't know if the need for honesty will get met. I refer to this period of time as tolerating the intolerable.

The book *Between a Rock and a Hard Place* chronicles the grueling account of Aron Ralston, an avid outdoorsman who was trapped by an 800-pound boulder in a Utah canyon in April 2003.

He was unable to sit, lie down, or move his right arm for six days. Running out of food and water, he eventually resorted to drinking his own urine to stave off dehydration. Ultimately, he was forced to amputate his arm with a dull, dirty pocketknife in order to escape and ultimately save his life. As horrific and as graphic as Aron's story is, it contains many parallels to a partner's experience of feeling trapped in an unbearable predicament—tolerating the intolerable.

Like Aron, you have experienced an unexpected and powerful trauma that seemingly came out of nowhere. You may have the ability to walk away from the situation, but many partners don't make that choice for a variety of good reasons. A long relationship history with the addict, a desire not to divorce, dependent children, financial vulnerability, and the hope that the relationship can be salvaged are some of the most common and compelling reasons partners choose to stay.

When you consider that honesty and trust are fundamental relationship needs, you may wonder how you can justify (to yourself) staying in a relationship that doesn't meet even the most basic of needs. As difficult as it is, there is a period of time when partners must tolerate the intolerable if they want to find out whether their relationship is salvageable. There is no way around this part of the recovery process and it can be extremely trying. You're between a rock and a hard place. It's excruciating, brutal, and it's survivable.

I like to use the metaphor of a funnel to describe the process addicts go through as they engage in healthier behaviors and become more transparent and honest. Imagine that the wide part at the top of the funnel is the time of early discovery and disclosure. During this time, the addict is dishonest and lies about many important things on a regular basis. He may also still be engaged in some, if not most, of his acting-out behaviors.

Moving down to the spout of the funnel the path becomes narrower—meaning the behaviors lessen and so does the dishonesty. The addict may not be honest 100 percent of the time, but the lies decrease and they're typically about issues that are less critical for the partner and the relationship. Granted, it's still not an ideal situation—but greatly improved. As the twelve-step slogan says, "Progress, not perfection."

As you navigate this painful phase, it's important to trust your intuition and surround yourself with supportive people who can help you maintain a sense of calm in the storm. Focus on getting your basic needs met, especially those you can meet yourself or that can be accomplished with the help of people other than the addict.

A PARTNER'S BILL OF RIGHTS

The fog of addiction causes partners' perception of their rights to be called into question and doubt. When you lose touch with a sense of your rights as a person or a partner, you will be confused about your needs. For example, if you've been told repeatedly that the sex addict's whereabouts are none of your business, or that all men look at porn and go to strip clubs, or that an affair partner is "just a friend"—when you know she is not—you will begin to believe the lies. Over time you will eventually let go of needs and forget that you have fundamental rights.

Below is a *Partner's Bill of Rights*. As you read them you may notice that although you agree with many or all of them, you struggle to claim them for yourself. The first Right is the Right to be Wrong. Why? Your intuition has and will continue to give you information about yourself, your partner, and your situation. More often than not your intuition is right, but sometimes it isn't and that's okay. Trust it anyway. If, with the passage of time or new information, you realize your intuition was wrong you can always change your mind—Right #2!

Partner's Bill of Rights
1. I have the right to be wrong.

2. I have the right to change my mind and change course.

3. I have the right to honesty in my primary relationship.

4. I have the right to expect my partner to honor our mutual agreements, commitments, and vows.

5. I have the right to say "no" to any request that feels uncomfortable physically, emotionally, sexually, or spiritually.

6. I have the right and the responsibility to protect my children from the addict's acting-out behaviors.

7. I have the right to take actions to protect myself physically, emotionally, sexually, or financially.

8. I have the right to request any reasonable behaviors or actions that will create safety and rebuild trust.

9. I have the right to be angry and to express my anger in appropriate and responsible ways.

10. I have the right to request a polygraph as part of a formal, therapeutic disclosure.

11. I have the right to full disclosure of the sex addict's sexual acting-out behaviors, money spent, and the extent to which my children may have been impacted by the addict's behaviors.

12. I have the right to request recovery check-ins and/or information about the addict's recovery activities and progress.

13. I have the right to request that the addict sleep in another room or live elsewhere for a period of time.

14. I have the right to receive proof or evidence that the addict has terminated a relationship and/or contact with an affair partner.

15. I have the right to request that the addict follow the recommendations of his therapist, sponsor, accountability partner, or clergy member.

16. I have the right to choose to have no contact with current or former affair partners regardless of their relationship to me or the addict (including family, coworkers, friends, or clergy).

17. I have the right to choose a boundary for myself regardless of the opinion of others.

Notice the many fundamental relationship needs mentioned in this list such as safety, protection, honesty, mutual respect, and communication (connection).

PARTNERS SPEAK

"Early on after I realized I was married to a sex addict, I don't think I ever gave much thought to my needs. I was so devastated and hurt. I thought I wasn't good enough. I was constantly asking myself, What's wrong with me? or How could I be so stupid not to know? His gaslighting and the crazy-making conversations we had finally drove me to the realization that I couldn't look to him as the only source of getting my needs met. This is when everything started to change for me."

—Lynn T.

CREATING A VISION OF NEEDS FULFILLED

The second and final part of Boundary Solution Step 2 is to create a vision of what it would look like if your need was fulfilled. In this step you're focused on your vision rather than the specific request you may eventually make to the sex addict.

Once you've identified the needs that aren't being fulfilled in your current situation, ask yourself, "What is the outcome I want, or what is my vision, with regard to this issue?" Your vision should be specific and measurable (for example: "I want my partner to call me once a day between 8:00 p.m. and 10:00 p.m. when he/she is out of town").

When thinking about your vision, don't limit yourself by starting with what you think is possible or what the sex addict will agree to. For this exercise, the sky is the limit. You may be thinking, *After all I've been through—all the disappointments, broken agreements, and deception—you want me to let myself dream?* Yes, that's exactly what I want you to do. Many partners have experienced so much repeated disappointment that their ability to imagine, dream, and envision a happier, more fulfilled life and relationship is severely damaged. Even if you don't think it's possible in your current relationship, it's important for you to give yourself the gift of asking yourself what you want. You have a right to dream and you have a right to want what you want. Wouldn't you rather aim for 1000 and get to 500 than aim for zero . . . and succeed?

Keep in mind that when you create a vision of needs fulfilled, the more clear, concrete, and measurable, the better. When it's clear and specific, you'll know when it has actually happened. For example, if you tell your partner you would like him to go to more twelve-step meetings, what does that mean? "More" is not specific and measurable. If he goes to four meetings in a month rather than the three he went to last month, that may not be what you had in mind! Your vision could be, "I would like my partner to go to three twelve-step meetings per week." This is a clear and measurable vision.

Below are some examples of clear, measurable outcomes a partner may want from the sex addict:

- Tell me when he's had a recovery slip within twenty-four to forty-eight hours of the slip.

- Attend a specified number of twelve-step meetings per week or per month.

- Stop all contact with former acting-out partners and provide proof of the communication.

- Change phone number or email address so that former acting-out partners can no longer contact him.

• Take polygraph exams at regular intervals for a specific period of time (for example, two to four years) to be determined after receiving the recommendations of therapist(s).

PARTNERS SPEAK

"When my therapist asked me what I wanted to see happen in my relationship, I didn't have an answer. I was so focused on stopping the pain that I didn't let myself think about much of anything beyond that. I was just surviving day to day, preoccupied with worrying about what might happen or what my wife was doing. The therapist's question helped me see that not only did I have a right to ask myself what I wanted, but that doing so would help me move beyond the stuck place I was in."

—Anonymous

Although the outcomes listed previously focus on what you would like from the addict, you can also use the 5-SBS process to identify boundaries you want to set with yourself.

For example, some partners choose to be celibate in their relationship for a period of time as a way of protecting themselves, learning more about their own sexuality, or because they have used sex in the past as a means to control the addict's sexual behaviors outside the relationship. Some partners find themselves repeatedly looking at pornography or websites the addict visited in the past to connect with potential or actual affair partners in an attempt to understand the addict, or to compare themselves to the people they see in personal ads, online profiles, or pornography. Although the initial intention may be to make sense of their world or to gain a sense of safety, over time partners find that these activities are painful and re-traumatizing.

Another boundary a partner may place on herself is to refrain from abusive behavior toward the addict. Some partners struggle with raging and even physical abuse of the addict. No matter what the addict has done, abuse of any kind is never justified.

Here are some common boundaries that partners place on themselves, and can be listed as an outcome in Boundary Solution Step 2:

- I will be celibate in my relationship and refrain from having sex with the addict for a specified period of time—thirty, sixty, or ninety days.

- I will not look at websites or social media the sex addict used to search for affair partners.

- I will not yell, rage, or curse at the sex addict when I become angry or fearful.

To complete Boundary Solution Step 2, review your reality from Step 1 and then identify the need or needs that aren't being met in your current situation. The needs list on the next page includes some of the most common individual and relationship needs for you to use as a starting point.

After you've identified the needs, write one clear, specific, and measurable outcome you are seeking. Remember, you can complete multiple "5-SBS Clarifiers" for various problems or issues for which you want to create boundaries.

■ EXERCISE

BOUNDARY SOLUTION STEP 2: IDENTIFY YOUR NEEDS AND CREATE YOUR VISION

Here is a list of common needs that might apply to your current reality as you identified it in Boundary Solution Step 1. What are the needs that are not currently being met with regard to this situation? On your "5-SBS Clarifier," note the two to three most important needs that stand out to you from the list below and add your own if necessary. A more comprehensive list of needs is provided in the Appendix.

○ Affection   ○ Authenticity/Genuineness

○ Autonomy/Independence   ○ Closeness/Touch

○ Communication   ○ Community

○ Companionship   ○ Freedom

○ Harmony   ○ Honesty

○ Mutuality/Give & Take   ○ Order/Reliability

○ Peace   ○ Respect

○ Safety   ○ Stability

○ Support   ○ Trust

The second part of Boundary Solution Step 2 is getting clear on the outcome you want by writing it down. Ask yourself, "What is the outcome I want, or what is my vision, with regard to this issue?" Your vision should be specific and measurable (for example, "I want my partner to call me once a day between 8:00 p.m. and 10:00 p.m. when he is out of town"). Enter your answer now in the "5-SBS Clarifier" before continuing to Chapter Six.

Now that you're clear about your needs and the outcome you want, how will you make it happen? The next step— Boundary Solution Step 3—is to determine where the power lies to get the results you want. Without knowing your power center, you will miss opportunities to take action where you have the power to do so, or you will waste valuable time and effort attempting to manage or control situations over which you have no control.

CHAPTER SIX

Boundary Solution Step 3: Identifying Your Power Center

PARTNERS SPEAK

"I thought I was standing in my power when I was demanding, raging, and physically abusive. But with each demand, each rage, and each physical attack, I felt shame. I realized I was totally powerless. I stopped focusing on him and focused, instead, on establishing boundaries for myself and changing my behaviors. That's when I truly stepped into my power."

—Jadine

POWER, AUTHENTIC POWER, AND "POWER OVER"

Power can be defined as the ability to do something or to act in a particular way, as well as the capacity to direct or influence the behavior of others or the course of events.

As you navigate through your healing process, you'll make smoother progress and avoid many pitfalls by understanding power—its uses as well as its abuses. Two of the most common mistakes partners, and most people, make is believing they don't have power, or believing they have power when they don't. When you don't recognize where you have power to affect change, you miss many opportunities to improve your life—both individually and relationally—and to get your needs met. On the other hand, when you mistakenly believe that you have power over people or situations when you don't, you create unnecessary frustration for yourself and waste precious time you could spend on more effective and productive activities and endeavors.

What is your relationship to power? Do you run away from it, secretly wish for it, or crave it? Most of us are unconscious, ambivalent, or conflicted about how we exercise power in our lives and relationships. For women, power can often have negative associations. Powerful women are sometimes perceived as cold, arrogant, or "bitches." Men also struggle around having a functional relationship with power. To be a powerful man may mean having status, wealth, or the ability to dominate or win—often through the use of control or force.

As a partner of a sex addict, you may often feel painfully powerless. If you are part of a twelve-step community, you're familiar with the first step of all twelve-step programs:

"We admitted we were powerless over _____."

In the case of sex addiction, you could fill in the blank with the sex addict, sex addiction, or simply addiction. In twelve-step programs focused on recovering from issues of codependency, the first step is, "We admitted we were powerless over others . . ." This is a motto we can all live by!

The idea of powerlessness can immobilize you if you believe you can't possibly stay with your partner if his behavior doesn't change. If you're powerless over the addict and you can't tolerate his current behavior, you will feel hopeless and helpless. You don't have power over the addict's behavior, choices, or thoughts. However, you *do* have power over how you respond to/what you do about situations and events in your life. This kind of power is what I call *authentic personal power*.

I often tell partners, "You have much more power than you realize," and this is almost always the case. In your ideal world, you would probably like to say just the right thing, make just the right threat, or, if all else fails, wave a magic wand and have your sex addict partner change his behavior so you can feel better. As wonderful as it would be to create this kind of immediate and lasting change—it's not going to happen. Believe it or not, you will feel better and ultimately more powerful when you truly accept that there is only one person over whom you have power, and that is you.

In the two definitions of power given at the beginning of this chapter, the first one describes "authentic power" while the second one describes "power over." Except in relationships where there is a clearly defined and agreed upon relationship hierarchy—such as employee/employer or teacher/student—no adult has the authority or power to direct the behavior of another person without that person's willing consent. "Power over" relies on the use of negative control, manipulation, coercion, intimidation, or force.

A person acting from a place of authentic personal power

- understands that she is the only person over whom she has control or power;

- is in touch with her needs and wants, and goes about getting them met in an honest and direct way;

- makes requests of others rather than issuing demands or ultimatums;

- is in touch with her inherent worth and value (in other words, esteems herself);

- is aware and accountable for the impact of her behavior on others;

- is clear, grounded, and centered;

- doesn't rely on manipulation, control, intimidation, force, or revenge to get her needs met;

- accepts powerlessness, when appropriate.

HOW PARTNERS LOSE POWER

The three most common ways partners of sex addicts lose power are by 1) taking a *head in the sand* approach, 2) engaging in subtle forms of control (also known as "enabling" behaviors), or 3) creating a kind of *sex addiction police state* inside the relationship with the sex addict.

If you take a *head in the sand* approach, you believe that

- it's his problem and he needs to fix it on his own;

- you don't need (or want) to know about his recovery plan;

- he needs to talk to his therapist, sponsor, or others about his struggles and his program—not you;

- you shouldn't ask him to go to meetings or therapy because he'll do it just to placate you;

- if you *have to* ask for trust-building or relationship repair behaviors, then his recovery isn't real or genuine.

Often, partners aren't necessarily opposed to knowing about the sex addict's recovery activities—it just doesn't occur to them to ask for the information.

Although I would never tell a partner that she *must* be informed or aware of the sex addict's recovery, there are definite problems with the *head in the sand* approach.

First, a hands-off stance mimics your pre-discovery relationship. The sex addict was leading a secret life of addiction of which you had no awareness. The difference now is that the "secret" life is his recovery.

Although on the surface taking a hands-off approach to the addict's recovery may appear to be healthy detachment, it can actually be a form of denial and/or avoidance. When you choose to let the addict's recovery and growth remain in a separate compartment from your connection as a couple, you miss a significant opportunity for relationship repair, healing, and intimacy. You also miss the opportunity to experience what it feels like to own your right—your authentic power—to ask for what you want.

When partners want little or no information, there are usually underlying reasons such as depression, learned helplessness, fear of intimacy, avoidance, high levels of anxiety, childhood neglect or abandonment, or in some cases, a secret romantic or sexual relationship. You may have never asked yourself what you want or need. You may have grown up in a family system where your needs and wants were neglected. It takes awareness, courage, and vulnerability to ask for what you need. Don't do to yourself today what was done to you in the past.

*"The most common way people give up their power
is by thinking they don't have any."*

—Alice Walker

The second way partners lose power is by engaging in subtle forms of influence or control through "offering help" to the sex addict by leaving self-help books around the home, asking indirect questions about his recovery activities, or suggesting he go to a twelve-step meeting. The partner may attempt to set up a therapy session for the addict or drive him to recovery meetings. These are all examples of indirect and ineffective strategies of control.

You may say, "But I'm only trying to help!" In recovery communities this kind of "help" is called enabling the addict or enabling addiction. These behaviors are enabling because they're attempts to take responsibility for his behavior, recovery, and the related consequences. Although they may seem innocent on the surface, they're examples of "power over" versus authentic personal power. Anytime you attempt to get someone else to do what you want him to do or influence him to behave in a certain way (usually to alleviate your own fear and anxiety), you're not standing in your authentic personal power.

The third way partners lose power is by creating a kind of *sex addiction police state* within the relationship with the addict. This is a "power over" strategy where partners go to great lengths to monitor or control the activities of the addict. Examples include:

- Being the accountability partner who monitors the addict's online activities (this is better handled by someone else, such as a program accountability partner).

- Demanding that the addict respond immediately to texts and phone calls at unreasonable times such as during business meetings, while driving, sleeping, attending family events, or taking care of young children.

- Monitoring or following the addict—in real time or online (on social media, in phone records, email accounts, etc.).

- Demanding that the addict give detailed or graphic descriptions of his thoughts, fantasies, and triggers.

- Directly telling the addict what to do, making demands, or issuing ultimatums instead of requests.

- Shaming and berating the addict.

- Abusing the addict emotionally or physically.

The problem with this approach is that it's not relational, and ultimately doesn't accomplish what the partner hopes it will. Even if you set up every available means of monitoring or controlling the addict's behavior, you realize that there is always the possibility that he has managed to avoid detection.

A sex addiction police state within a relationship sets up an unhealthy and toxic power dynamic between you and the sex addict. Your role in his life is now that of an authority figure, consequence maker, and adversary rather than companion, partner, and lover. If your goal is to have a healthy, connected, and intimate relationship, you won't get there through hypervigilance, control, or punishment.

"Power over" strategies, including enabling and direct control, are nonrelational means to regain a sense of safety or control by someone who feels helpless and powerless. Although they're tempting strategies and sometimes work in the short term, they're not long-term solutions. Over time, they can lead to more disconnection, power struggles, resentment, and even relapse for the addict if he allows his partner to control or abuse him without setting boundaries.

VANISH THE VICTIM

As a partner of a sex addict, there is no doubt that you've been victimized. Any time there is a boundary violation, there is the possibility of victimization. Repeated deception, gaslighting, and crazy-making behaviors are some of the most insidious forms of victimizing another person. The good news is that once you become aware that you've been deceived and betrayed, you have the choice and the power to protect yourself from further victimization.

Partners sometimes get stuck in a victim mindset, taking on the identity of a victim rather than a person who *was* victimized. A persistent or fixed belief that you're a victim is a dangerous attitude that reinforces a "power over" approach that is ultimately disempowering.

Except in rare circumstances like unjust imprisonment or being held against your will, the experience of victimization lasts only a brief time. After the actual event of being victimized, you are no longer a victim in the present moment. When you're free to choose your response, you are not a victim.

Being a victim is a state of mind, rather than a circumstance. Many people who are victimized, even in horrific ways, rise above their circumstances. They may have survived abuse or discrimination but they don't identify as victims. Nelson Mandela, Mahatma Gandhi, and Viktor Frankl are all well-known role models who exemplify the reality that circumstances don't have to make someone a victim.

If your partner is irresponsible about handling money and you choose to separate your money from his, this constitutes a boundary and an act of protection. You may believe that you're a victim because you tell yourself that you *had to* create the boundary because of your partner's irresponsibility. This is not true. Among the many choices you could have made—including doing nothing—you chose to separate the money.

> Don't cripple your ability to practice
> good self-care by equating self-protection
> with being a victim.

It may be hard to hear, but victim thinking is actually self-centered. If you're stuck in a victim mindset, you feel one down, helpless, and at the mercy of others. From this place you perceive yourself as the target of unfortunate events and other people. You may interpret random events as being about your exceptionally bad luck or as a sign that other people are out to get you. You become "terminally unique" in your outlook and you may even become paranoid. When you take on the role of victim as an identity or a badge of honor, you are actively participating in your victimization and disowning your authentic personal power.

"You are only a victim for a nanosecond."

—Pia Mellody

One of the most dangerous aspects of perceiving yourself as a victim is that you begin to believe you have a right to victimize others. Pia Mellody calls this "offending from the victim position." When you offend from the victim position you tell yourself that the other person has victimized you in some way, which may or may not be true. Perceiving yourself as a victim, you feel one down and powerless. You believe you have a right to retaliate or to take revenge—in essence, play God or another person's Higher Power.

If your boundary has been violated you *do* have a right to be angry and to set a boundary. However, you don't have a right to offend and retaliate. I've witnessed many partners who justify outrageous and offensive behaviors, including physical abuse of the sex addict, by telling themselves that their partner deserved it because of his behavior. If you experience repetitive boundary violations in a relationship, you must learn how to tap into your power to decide how best to protect yourself. If you don't protect yourself, you become a victim of your choice to not take action.

The fundamental problem with offending from the victim position is that you justify violating another person's boundaries because he or she violated (or you perceive he or she violated) yours. If I have a right to hit my partner because he lied to me, then do I have a right to break his arm if he's unfaithful, or kill him if he was unfaithful with my best friend? This is offending from the victim position taken to an extreme. It's the practice of "power over" rather than authentic personal power. If your response to boundary violations is motivated by punishment, revenge, and retaliation, you have lost sovereignty over yourself; you have had a failure of character and integrity.

In the short term, "power over" *does* get results—in the same way an intimidating person wielding a weapon can get results. "Power over" can feel empowering and even exhilarating in the moment. But in the long term it's toxic and destructive to your relationship.

Stepping out of the victim role requires the following four steps:

1. Making a choice to be victorious over your problem rather than a victim or a volunteer.

2. Identifying where you have power.

3. Letting go of what you're powerless over.

4. Taking action where you have power.

Cultivating a sense of your own authentic personal power will change you—and your relationships—forever. When you're clear about what is in your power to change and what isn't, you will be much more effective at going about getting your needs met. You won't waste time attempting to change people and situations over which you have no control. You will learn to focus on your goals, what you want and need, and your own reality rather than trying to figure out other people.

> *"Make the best use of what is in your power,*
> *and take the rest as it happens."*
>
> *—Epictetus*

When two people in a relationship are aware of and know how to use authentic personal power, they are able to share power. They recognize and honor the right of the other to ask for what they need and they work to avoid power struggles—trying to be right or "win." They are also able to tolerate the discomfort that arises when the other person has a different opinion or perception. They don't have a need to change the other person's mind or to make them into someone other than who they are. This doesn't mean accepting abusive or offensive behavior.

When a relationship is operating at this level, neither person has a need to manipulate, coerce, or pressure the other. Each one is clear and direct in the expression of his or her wants and needs and knows how to make requests, negotiate, and compromise.

Examples of sharing power in relationships impacted by sex addiction include the following:

- Collaborative transparency, where you and the sex addict create agreements about access to the addict's personal belongings such as phone, computer, or email accounts.

- Clear, mutually acceptable agreements, for example, regarding couples' check-ins.

- Addict understands and participates in relationship repair and rehabilitation as an opportunity for growth and healing rather than an obligation or punishment.

- Partner understands her needs and makes appropriate requests.

- Addict sets limits on controlling and/or abusive behavior by partner.

COLLABORATIVE TRANSPARENCY

Collaborative transparency is a process where the sex addict is forthcoming and transparent about his activities and behaviors based on agreements made between the addict and the partner. Collaborative transparency requires both partner and sex addict to work together to create a framework for rebuilding trust and repairing the relationship.

The process begins with you, as the partner, identifying—specifically—what you would like the addict to do (or refrain from doing) to repair the damage done to the relationship and help you to begin to trust again. Requests may include attending twelve-step meetings; sharing passwords for email, phone, and credit card accounts; formal therapeutic disclosure; or taking a baseline polygraph or follow-up polygraphs (after formal therapeutic disclosure).

After creating a list of trust-building behaviors, you then make requests directly to the addict. The addict honestly assesses whether he can agree to what you request. The addict either 1) agrees, 2) doesn't agree, or 3) offers an alternative solution to which he can agree. You must keep in mind that if you can't accept "no" from the addict, then his "yes" will have little meaning at best, or will become a future broken agreement at worst.

Once the agreements are made, the couple writes them down in an agreement or contract journal, signs, and dates them. Recording agreements in writing creates clear communication, accountability, and a resource for future reference if needed. (How to make effective requests, along with more details about use of a couples' agreement journal is covered in Chapter Seven.)

YOUR HIGHER POWER

No discussion of power is complete without addressing your Higher Power, God, the Divine, or however you define Higher Power for yourself. If you have a relationship with a Higher Power, this is an excellent time to nurture this relationship. Now, more than ever, you need spiritual support and guidance. If you're agnostic or atheist, you may relate more to the concept of a wise or higher Self, or rely on friends, family, and your community for guidance and support.

There are times when we are powerless to create the outcome that we want. At those times, calling on your Higher Power and knowing that others also have a Higher Power, can help you let go of people and situations over which you have no power. Experiences of powerlessness and unmanageability are often the catalyst that drives us—sometimes kicking and screaming—to a closer connection with our Higher Power.

When you're powerless, the only actions you can take are to let go, pray, and offer the problem to a power greater than yourself. Surrendering to the reality that you're powerless over people, places, and things offers a sense of peace and freedom that will remain elusive so long as you're working hard to control what is ultimately not in your control.

Sometimes, a partner attempts to become the Higher Power of the other. In relationships impacted by sex addiction and betrayal, the betrayed partner may place herself in the position of a Higher Power toward the sex addict by using strategies of "power over" or control. This is not workable for you or your relationship.

One of the symptoms of love addiction—a severe form of codependency—is that the love addict puts her partner on a pedestal and makes her partner her Higher Power. In practical terms, this means that the love addict will look to her partner as her primary and perhaps only source of esteem, happiness, and love. Not surprisingly, this makes the love addict quite vulnerable in her relationship since her sense of value and power rises and falls depending on what her partner is doing, or not doing. In addition, the love addict is in a perpetual state of feeling "less than" in the relationship, having made her partner her Higher Power. This dynamic is toxic to relationships.

To strengthen your connection to your Higher Power, you may want to become re-engaged or more deeply involved with your church, synagogue, temple, or mosque. Or it may be time to explore new spiritual practices or spiritual/religious communities. Through prayer or meditation, ask your Higher Power for guidance and be open to the information you receive. When you're tempted to use "power over" strategies of manipulation or control, gently remind yourself that you are not the addict's (or anyone else's) Higher Power, and that your partner also has a Higher Power.

IDENTIFY YOUR POWER CENTER

Once you've identified your reality, the needs that aren't being met in the current situation, and what you'd like the ideal outcome to look like, you need to determine where the power to change the situation lies. In identifying where you have power, there are four possible options:

1. You have the power to create the outcome you want.

2. You have the power to create the outcome you want, with help.

3. You must make a request of another person in order to create the outcome you want.

4. You are powerless over creating the outcome you want.

The first option is the simplest, in that you have the power to create the outcome you want. For example, if you would like to sleep separately from your partner for a period of time, you have the power to do that. Or, if you are concerned about your partner's use of money, you can open a separate bank account to protect funds that rightfully belong to you.

The second option is that you have the power to create the outcome, but you need help in order to make it happen. For example, if you want to go to couples' therapy and the addict has agreed to go with you, you need the help of a therapist (in the form of an appointment) to accomplish your goal.

The third option—making a request—requires that you get agreement from another person to accomplish the outcome you want. For example, if you want your partner to reduce the number of out-of-town business trips he takes for a period of time, the only way you can get this outcome is if your partner agrees. The difference between option 2 and 3 is that option 3 requires the agreement of another person. These are the kinds of boundary issues that typically create the most conflict and distress. They are also most likely to result in future boundary challenges such as broken agreements, boundary violations, and disappointment due to lack of follow-through—sometimes on the part of both people involved in the agreement.

The last option is powerlessness. There are many things over which we are powerless including

- anything that happened in the past;

- situations, relationships, or people with whom we don't have the ability to make a request;

- what another person thinks or fantasizes about.

As frustrating as it can be to realize that you are powerless over the outcome you want, it can also be clarifying and freeing. Some partners spend months or years attempting to get the addict into recovery. If the partner is doing her own individual work, she will eventually face the reality that the addict is not willing to do the work necessary to change, and this becomes a relationship deal-breaker for her. As sad and disappointed as she may be, when she accepts that she can't make the addict engage in recovery or change him in any way, she will experience relief and even joy for having let go of the struggle and repeated disappointment of trying to make him be or do something he wasn't willing to be or do.

It's essential to understand how power works and to be clear about where your power lies before proceeding to Boundary

Solution Step 4, where you'll create and implement an action plan. If you mistakenly believe you don't have the power to change your situation, get help, or make requests of others, you'll miss an important opportunity to practice self-care and get your needs met—creating more clarity and serenity in your life. On the other hand, if you attempt to take action in a situation over which you have no power, you will waste precious time and energy. You will also experience more frustration than necessary and potentially delay your healing process.

Take some time now to complete Boundary Solution Step 3 on the "5-SBS Clarifier."

■ EXERCISE

BOUNDARY SOLUTION STEP 3: IDENTIFY YOUR POWER CENTER

Do you have the power to create the result you want without asking for help or making a request? If not, can you create the result you want with help from someone else, or does the result require making a request of another person? Are you powerless to create the result? On the "5-SBS Clarifier," identify and take note of all that apply:

> *I have the power to create*
> *I need help*
> *I need to make a request*
> *I am powerless*

CHAPTER SEVEN

Boundary Solution Step 4: Creating and Implementing Your Action Plan

"The number one reason that we don't get our needs met, we don't express them. We express judgments. If we do express needs, the number two reason we don't get our needs met, we don't make clear requests."

—*Marshall Rosenberg*

Now that you know the difference between authentic power, "power over," and powerlessness, it's time to move to Boundary Solution Step 4—creating and implementing your action plan. This is the step where the clarity you've gained from knowing your reality and your understanding of where your power lies join forces to help you create the outcome you want.

THE FOUR POSSIBLE ACTIONS

There are four possible actions you can take to create an outcome, or to release it if you're powerless to make it happen. You'll notice that each potential action is based on what you identified as your Power Center in Boundary Solution Step 3. Here are the four possible actions:

1. Do what needs be done to create the outcome you want (when it's in your power to do so).

2. Ask for help.

3. Make a request.

4. Do nothing.

We will cover each of these in detail.

Before you decide which action(s) to take, you need to have an understanding of the following key concepts to help you create your action plan:

• Contracts and Expectations

• Demands, Ultimatums, and Requests

• Non-negotiable Boundaries

CONTRACTS AND EXPECTATIONS

CONTRACT
A written or spoken agreement.

EXPECTATION
A strong belief that something will happen in the future.

Knowing the difference between an expectation and a contract is essential for good boundary work. In relationships, we create expectations based on our own thoughts, or on what we've assumed or made up about what others will or won't do. Sometimes, we create expectations that reflect what we want to happen rather than the reality of the situation.

People often make the mistake of believing they have a contract (or agreement) with someone when in reality they've created an expectation of what the other person will or won't do. For example, if a friend says she plans to go to a music festival next Friday night and you decide to go, you might expect to see her there. If she's not there, you may be disappointed because you would have liked to see her. However, since she didn't make a commitment (agreement/contract) to you directly, the fact that she didn't go to the festival doesn't constitute a broken agreement.

On the other hand, if your friend says, "I'm going to the music festival Friday night. Would you like to meet me there at 8:00 p.m.?" and you agree to meet her, then the two of you have an agreement, or contract. If either of you don't show up, then the contract was broken and a boundary violation has occurred.

If an expectation is based on a commitment made directly by another person to do something for us or with us, then it's a contract. For example, if the sex addict says he will call you if he's going to be more than fifteen minutes late coming home from work, he has a contract with you. If he doesn't follow through with the commitment, then the contract has been broken.

If you believe you have a contract (agreement) with the sex addict, but it's only an expectation, you will feel angry, let down, and disappointed when he doesn't do what you expected. The problem isn't that the addict didn't do what you wanted or expected. The problem lies with your misunderstanding of the difference between contracts and expectations.

When you make a request of another person, you don't have a contract or agreement unless you get a direct, affirmative response. One of the best ways to make an agreement or create a contract with the sex addict partner is to make requests. Requests take vulnerability and courage. You're taking a risk in asking for what you want, and you're also taking the risk that you may not get what you request.

Understanding the difference between expectations and contracts will help you identify broken agreements, boundary violations, and avoid misunderstandings and unnecessary pain.

DEMANDS, ULTIMATUMS, AND REQUESTS

There are many ways of asking for—and getting—what you want and need from another person. The possibilities range from passive, indirect methods to the other extreme of using intimidation, threats, or direct force. The difference between demands, ultimatums, and requests isn't well understood—even by people who have some awareness of effective communication and boundaries.

DEMAND

A forceful statement in which you say that something must be done or given to you.

ULTIMATUM

A final demand or statement of terms, the rejection of which will result in retaliation or a breakdown in relations.

REQUEST

An act of asking politely, respectfully, or formally for something.

Most people are on the passive or indirect end of the continuum when it comes to getting their needs and wants met. The passive approach sounds like, "It sure is hot in here," when what you would really like is for the other person to turn down the temperature on the thermostat. A more direct—and relational— way to communicate this need is, "I'm feeling warm; would you be willing to turn the thermostat down a few degrees?"

On the other end of the continuum, you may make demands or tell others what to do. Some couples routinely speak to one another this way. For example, "Get me a glass of water," or "Get off the phone," or worse, "You can't go out with your friends tonight, I need you to stay here and help me with some paperwork from the office"—these are all demands rather than requests.

Making demands assumes that we have the rightful authority to tell another person what to do. In healthy relationships, complaints and serious concerns are communicated as requests rather than demands or ultimatums. No matter what we may "demand" of someone, we are powerless over whether the demand is met. And worse, demands are destructive and toxic to adult relationships.

One of the most common mistakes partners make when they begin doing boundary work is telling the addict what he should or shouldn't do. When talking about boundaries, partners often say things like, "I set my boundaries," or "I told him my boundaries," when what they're really saying is that they told the sex addict what he will do. It is perfectly understandable that you believe you have a right to expect your partner to cut off contact with an affair partner or to allow you to have access to his phone. However, you're practicing "power over" rather than using authentic personal power in the form of boundary work when you make demands rather than requests.

A healthy boundary expresses what one will and will not accept in a relationship, and clearly states how the person setting the boundary will practice self-care if the boundary is violated. You can tell the addict what *you* will do if he chooses to continue contact with an affair partner or won't allow you access to his phone, but you can't get your needs met by telling him what he will or won't do.

You may be wondering, "Aren't there exceptions for outrageous behaviors like sexual infidelity? Shouldn't I be able to tell him that he has to stop what he's doing?" The short answer is no. Of course, if you and your partner have a prior commitment to monogamy, your partner has violated the commitment. Your options are to either request that he recommit to the prior agreement, or take another action (for example, ask him to go to couples' therapy, separate, or divorce). Even in relationships that have been devastated by sexual betrayal, ultimatums and demands may work in the short term, but they are ultimately ineffective and destructive to the relationship.

> You have power over what you can do
> yourself and the requests you choose to
> make in your relationships.

Ultimatums are threats made in the form of a demand. If the demand isn't met, the consequence is usually retaliation, or the end of a relationship. In intimate relationships, ultimatums are attempts at creating a certain outcome by getting the other person to do what you want them to do. The person expressing the ultimatum is often not prepared or willing to follow through with the stated consequence. The message underlying most ultimatums is, "I'm angry and terrified. You better _____ (stop acting out, stop lying, go to therapy, etc.), so I won't have to feel this pain. If you don't, I will punish you by _____."

Here is an example of a boundary a partner may set that could be interpreted as an ultimatum: "I need you to honor our agreement to be sexually faithful to me. If you have sex with another person again, I will leave the relationship."

This is a non-negotiable relationship boundary. A non-negotiable boundary can sound very much like an ultimatum. In fact, the boundary above might be an ultimatum if the partner's sole intention is to influence the sex addict's behavior by threatening to leave. If this is the partner's only intention in stating the boundary, she probably won't follow through. On the other hand, if the partner's intention is to let the addict know what she will do if the boundary is broken, then the above statement is a non-negotiable relationship boundary.

An ultimatum is an attempt to control
another person's behavior.

A boundary is an expression of how you
plan to act or take care of yourself.

The sex addict may interpret this boundary—"If you have sex with another person again I will leave the relationship"—as an ultimatum. However, the partner isn't telling the sex addict what to do. She is not making a demand or a request. She's letting him know that if he chooses to have sex with someone else in the future, she will leave the relationship. This is a clear and relational statement of a boundary. The sex addict may believe this non-negotiable boundary is unreasonable. This is distorted, victim thinking. She has a right to set boundaries and he has a right to choose his actions.

HOW TO MAKE EFFECTIVE REQUESTS

Out of anger, fear, or attempts to control, partners frequently make demands rather than requests. They also set non-negotiable boundaries they later realize are unrealistic or too severe. When you're in pain and your life feels out of control, issuing a demand can provide a temporary feeling of relief and a momentary sense of power.

Here are some examples of demands partners may make and how to turn them into relational requests:

DEMANDS	REQUESTS
You have to check in with me every time you leave the office to go to a meeting or lunch.	I would like you to text me if you leave your office to go to a meeting or lunch and let me know where you're going. Would you be willing to do that?
You're going to take a follow-up polygraph every six months.	I want you to take a follow-up polygraph every six months. Is that something you'd be willing to do?
You can't go to any co-ed twelve-step meetings.	I feel afraid and anxious when you go to co-ed twelve-step meetings. I'd like you to go to men's/women's only meetings. Would you be willing to do that?

Each of these requests is clear, specific, and relational. Your partner can answer with yes, no, or negotiate an alternative agreement.

Making requests takes courage and vulnerability.

What if you make a request and the answer is no? That is always a risk when you ask for what you want. But ultimately, asking for what you want is the surest and quickest route to finding out if you're in a relationship that has potential for rehabilitation, or whether it is one that won't be healthy or fulfilling for you in the long term. If the addict says no to your request, he is giving you more information about his level of commitment to healing, recovery, and the relationship. This is one of the reasons why effective boundary work helps you determine whether or not your relationship is salvageable. You will need to determine what his choice means to you, and what you need to do to take care of yourself.

PARTNERS SPEAK

"Everyone at the meetings kept saying I needed to stay on my side of the street and focus on me. But she kept doing the same things—slipping, acting out, and lying. She promised me over and over that she would go to therapy but she didn't. It was hard to focus on me when I was so angry and miserable living with someone who didn't seem to care about my feelings or our relationship.

"Finally, I got my own therapist and he told me that it was perfectly okay for me to ask my partner to go to therapy, twelve-step meetings, or anything else I wanted to ask for that would help me begin to trust and want to stay in the relationship. I thought I couldn't ask for anything because that would be getting on her side of the street. Once I started asking for what I wanted, things started to get better. Not because I got everything I wanted, but because I was speaking up and also not putting up with things that didn't feel good. It didn't go perfectly, but I started to get how boundaries work."

—Anonymous

BEST PRACTICES FOR PRESENTING A REQUEST

Once you've decided what you want to request of your partner, you need to identify the most skillful way of doing so. Remember—your intention is to express your needs and wants, and to create an agreement. You're not trying to control, manipulate, prove something, or be right.

You will maximize the likelihood of being heard, and possibly getting an agreement, by following some simple dos and don'ts.

Do:

- Choose a time when the two of you are relatively calm and there are minimal distractions.

- Notice any physiological signs (such as rapid heart rate, sweaty palms, flushed/red skin) indicating that you may not be calm enough to have a productive conversation.

- Ask your partner if he's available to talk about something important.

- Be willing to take no for an answer and schedule another time to talk if your partner isn't available to talk when you ask him.

- Use relational questions such as

    - "I would like _____. Would you be willing to do that?"

    - "What I would like is _____. Is that something you're willing to do?"

    - "Would you be willing to _____?"

- Remember that your highest intention is to be intimate with your partner by sharing who you are, and to rebuild connection and trust.

Don't:

- Present your request when you're feeling highly activated or triggered. ("Activation" is a physical and emotional experience of feeling tense, edgy, or charged up in a non-sexual way. Feeling activated can range in intensity from very mild to severe. Because the word "triggered" is often associated with addicts' and partners' responses to people and/or events related to the addiction, I prefer the more general term "activation" when discussing experiences that may or may not be related to the addict or the addiction.)

- Present your request when you feel you must talk about the topic *now* and can't take no for an answer.

- Persist in talking to the addict when he says he's not in a good frame of mind to have a conversation.

- Insist on resolving the question immediately when your partner wants some time to think it over.

Finally, it can be helpful to ask yourself how much the particular request you're making matters to you. The more important the issue is to you, the more attached you will be to the outcome. I often ask clients to rate issues on a scale of one to ten, ten being the highest, most important, or powerful. You can use this ten-point scale to determine how important a request is to you. This simple rating question can be helpful in clarifying your thoughts and understanding your level of investment in an outcome. I also recommend this rating tool to help you decide how to respond when boundary violations occur, which we discuss more in Chapter Eight.

If you rate the issue higher than a six, your attachment to the outcome is strong. In this case it is helpful to be mindful of your attachment, and to consider sharing this with your partner. For example, you can say, "I am very attached to the outcome of this request. I really want you to do what I'm asking you to do. However, I know you have a right to say yes, no, or negotiate, and that I don't have a right to get everything I want."

PARTNER'S CHALLENGES TO TAKING ACTION

Sometimes partners struggle to take action in Step 4 and there are several possible reasons. Here are the most common:

- Issues of esteem and worth

- Family and financial considerations

- Overvaluing the relationship or the addict

- Trauma (family of origin and preexisting adult trauma)

- Situations of domestic abuse

If any of these apply to you, there is no need to berate yourself or create undue pressure to make something happen before you're absolutely sure of your choices. When we're under stress, depressed, or anxious, we get tunnel vision and have difficulty seeing that there are many more options than we realize.

We cover each of these and many other barriers to successful boundary work in Chapter Nine, along with recommendations for next steps. If your boundary work regularly comes to a halt at Step 4, you may need to address one or more of these issues before proceeding.

IMPLEMENTING YOUR ACTION PLAN

Now you're ready to create your action plan! Based on your answers in Boundary Solution Step 3: Identify Your Power Center, you will do one of the following:

1. If you have the power to create the outcome, do what needs to be done to make it happen.

If taking action on your own gets the job done, this is by far the easiest solution. For example, if you want to sleep separately from your partner for a temporary period of time and you prefer to sleep in another bedroom, you have the power to make that happen. This outcome is achievable without the need for help or making a request. Other examples of actions partners take for their own self-care include limiting contact with the addict when interactions are needlessly tense or crazy making, participating in hobbies, rewarding activities, or connecting with support communities to meet your needs for companionship, meaning, or safety.

Be sure to check yourself for potential resentments or victim thinking if you choose to take action to create the outcome. For example, if you're frustrated that the addict is spending several evenings a week at twelve-step meetings or engaged in other recovery activities, you will unknowingly disempower yourself if you believe you "had to" take up a new hobby to fill the time you would ordinarily spend with your partner.

> Taking action is an empowering choice, and where there is choice—with knowledge of the facts—it is impossible to be a victim.

Lastly, if the action you need to take is a challenge or a stretch for you, set a deadline to complete it and tell someone—friend, sponsor, therapist, or mentor—about your commitment so that you have accountability in place.

2. *If you need help to create the outcome you want, ask for help.*

Sometimes we need to ask for help in order to accomplish our goals. Many people struggle to ask for help; yet doing so can save you an enormous amount of time, energy, money, and even heartache. You may need to do some research to find the right person—a financial consultant, attorney, therapist, or physician, for example—or you may need to schedule an appointment of some kind. If you want to separate your money from your partner's, you might research where you'd like to set up a new account and go to the bank to open it. You might schedule a time to meet with a friend, mentor, sponsor, or therapist to help you figure out your next steps or to create a plan for disclosure or therapeutic separation. Outline the steps you need to take to get help and set deadlines. Consider putting some accountability in place to help support you in following through.

3. *Make a request.*

If the outcome you want requires that the addict engage—or not engage—in a particular behavior or activity, you can choose to make a request. Making and negotiating requests is one of the most confusing and challenging aspects of the boundary process, especially in relationships impacted by sex addiction.

As previously discussed, partners tend to default toward one end of the continuum or the other regarding making requests. Some partners don't request anything of the addict because they don't realize they have a right to, or they believe that making requests is the same as telling the addict what to do or attempting to run the addict's recovery. Partners on the other end of the continuum make demands or tell the addict what he can or can't do.

A request should never be interpreted as telling another person what to do. A request is essentially a question, and the person receiving a request has at least four options in how to respond. He can say yes or no, negotiate the request, or completely ignore it. Of course, ignoring a request is not respectful or relational, and should only be used in rare situations when someone is being intrusive or offensive in some way. When it comes to requests, the truth is that you can ask anyone for anything! However, it's always helpful to keep in mind that you may or may not get what you request. The possibility of the other person saying no to our requests makes the process an intimate and vulnerable experience.

Requests must be specific, clear, and measurable. Vague agreements create misunderstandings and future conflict. "Would you come home from the office by 6:00 p.m.?" is much clearer than "Would you come home on time?" If the request involves a deadline of some kind (taking a polygraph or completing disclosure, for example), it's best to set up a time frame such as, "By the end of the month" or "Within three weeks." When you make a request and create an agreement, there should be little, if any, doubt about whether or not the agreement was fulfilled.

If you want the sex addict to call more often when he's traveling, a specific request would be: "When you're traveling, I would like you to call me at least once a day, preferably at night after 8:00 p.m. when the children have gone to bed." This request is more effective than, "I want you to call me more when you're out of town." The latter request isn't specific or measurable, and there is no way to determine whether or not the request was met.

Lastly, remember that non-negotiable physical or sexual boundaries do not require a request. For example, if you don't want to be touched physically or sexually, or you don't want to be touched physically or sexually in a particular way, you have a right to say so without the need to make a request. Regarding non-negotiable physical or sexual boundaries, a no is a no.

EXAMPLES OF REQUESTS MADE BY PARTNERS OF SEX ADDICTS

- Participate in recovery activities such as twelve-step meetings, individual therapy, group therapy, workshops, intensive outpatient programs, or inpatient treatment (if recommended by a therapist).

- Follow the recommendations of your therapist, sponsor, accountability partner, or clergy member.

- Disclose to me immediately any information that puts my safety, health, financial security, or reputation at risk.

- Disclose to me immediately any information that puts the health or safety of our children at risk.

- Make a full disclosure (facilitated by a therapist trained in formal therapeutic disclosure protocols) of your sexual acting-out behaviors, money spent, and the extent to which my/our children may have been impacted by your addictive behaviors.

- Take a polygraph as part of a formal, therapeutic disclosure.

- Take follow-up polygraphs for some period of time determined by consultation with your mentor, sponsor, therapist, and/or clergy person.

- Provide weekly (or other timeframe) recovery check-ins and/or information about your recovery activities and progress.

- Sleep in another room or live elsewhere for a specified period of time.

- Proof or evidence that you have terminated relationships and/or contact with affair partners.

- Provide receipts or other evidence of cash spent (specifically for sex addicts who spent money on sexual acting out).

- Use phone app or other available electronic means to verify your whereabouts for a specified period of time.

YOUR PARTNER'S RIGHTS WHEN RECEIVING A REQUEST

When receiving a request, adults always have a right to say yes or no. Before discovery or disclosure, many partners went along with what the addict wanted them to do, and didn't realize they had a right to say no or didn't exercise their right. In recovery, partners sometimes have the mistaken belief that the sex addict must agree to everything she wants him to do. In personal relationships, no adult has the right to tell another adult what to do, no matter what the other person has done.

When presented with a request, a person has three possible choices about how to respond:

1. Agree to the request.

2. Negotiate the request.

3. Say no to the request.

If your partner agrees to the request, I recommend you write your agreements in an agreement journal. Write down each agreement, in detail, date the agreement, and initial or sign it. While it may seem unnecessary or rigid to keep an agreement journal, it's not uncommon for either the partner or addict to forget, or to have different recollections about agreements they've made. If you decide at a future time you no longer want or need the agreement, you can simply cross it off the list, initial, and date it. For example:

DATE _____

AGREEMENT
Adam agrees that he will call Judy each night between 9:00 p.m. and 10:00 p.m. when he is out of town.

SIGNED _____   _____
                ADAM   JUDY

The second option when receiving a request is to negotiate. For example, in the agreement above where Adam agreed to call Judy each night between 9:00 p.m. and 10:00 p.m. when he's out of town, Adam may realize that making this agreement isn't practical for him because he prefers to talk to Judy right before he goes to bed at 10:30 p.m. Adam can tell Judy that this is his preference and the two of them can decide together if Adam's preference is workable for Judy.

The third possible response—a no—is a firm boundary set by the other person. Partners often become confused about what to do when the addict says no to a request—much like when an agreement is broken or a boundary is violated. A knee-jerk response is to engage in an argument with the other person, tell them they're not being reasonable, or ask them why they're not willing to do what we're asking.

When your partner says no to a request, there are several ways you can respond. You can initiate a negotiation process to create an agreement. In the example above, if Adam says no to the request, Judy could ask him what he *is* willing to do. Another option is to revise the request. For example, Judy could revise the original request and ask, "Would you be willing to call sometime before you go to sleep?" A third option is to simply accept his answer of no.

If your partner says no to your request in Boundary Solution Step 4 and the request or the issue is very important to you, you can return to Steps 1–3 based on your new situation. The new data for Boundary Solution Step 1: Identify Your Reality is that your partner didn't agree to call you between 9:00 p.m. and 10:00 p.m. when he's out of town. You would then proceed to Steps 2 and 3, then return to Step 4 to create a new action plan.

4. Do nothing.

Doing nothing is sometimes the best possible action to take. You may be powerless to create the outcome you want, or you come to the realization that doing nothing is the best option for your self-care and healing. If you're powerless, you must find a way to let go and release the outcome.

Doing nothing—or accepting powerlessness—can feel like giving up, losing, or even failing. However, making the choice to do nothing is an action in itself. As paradoxical as it may seem, doing nothing is sometimes the most empowered choice you can make even though it can appear passive on the surface. Remember that when you've made the choice to do nothing or take no action, you have freely made the choice and are therefore not a victim.

The second situation in which doing nothing is the best option is when you've made multiple attempts to get your needs met (using the tools in the 5-SBS), and you haven't gotten the result you want due to repeated broken agreements, boundary violations, or other factors. As Albert Einstein famously remarked, it is insane to continue doing the same thing while hoping for a different outcome. Stopping the insanity sometimes requires us to accept powerlessness and let go.

Lastly, you may choose to do nothing in situations where you realize that taking an action will create a response or a result that is unpleasant for you or one that you want to avoid. For example, if the addict becomes defensive or hostile when you bring up issues that are relatively unimportant to you or don't impact you directly, you may choose not to make a request because the benefit you might get from making the request doesn't offset the negative consequences of asking. Having said that, doing nothing would clearly not be a viable option if there is ongoing emotional, physical, or sexual abuse.

Choosing not to take action is often the best option when the issue is merely a difference of opinion or a different style of getting something done. For example, there is no right or wrong way to do many things, including loading a dishwasher, driving from point A to point B, cleaning, organizing, or planning a vacation. When differences like these arise, taking the high road and allowing for differences is usually the best, although not always the easiest, choice.

A word of caution about doing nothing: Before you decide to let go of a particular issue, honestly assess how important it is to you by rating the problem on a scale of one to ten, ten being of the highest importance. If you rate the issue above a six, and the only way you can get the need met is to make a request, then doing nothing is probably not an empowered or caring option for you, and may create future resentment.

Take some time now to complete Boundary Solution Step 4 on the "5-SBS Clarifier" and create your action plan.

■ EXERCISE

BOUNDARY SOLUTION STEP 4: TAKE ACTION

Based on your answer to Boundary Solution Step 3, do one of the following:

1. *I have the power to create the outcome*: What I need to do to create the desired outcome: _____. I will complete this Step by (date): _____.

2. *I need to ask for help*: Seek help from _____ to create the desired outcome. I will complete this Step by (date):

   _____.

3. *I need to make a request*: What is the specific request I need to make? Ask the person if they are willing to _____ (the request must be *measurable* and *clear*. For example, "I would like you to give me all of your receipts for cash spent on Friday each week for the next three months. Would you be willing to do that?" rather than "Would you be willing to give me your receipts?"). If agreed on (and applicable), this Step will be completed by (date): _____.

4. *Do nothing*: Release the problem because you're powerless to change it, or choose to do nothing because doing nothing is the best course of action (provided you can make this choice without believing you're a victim).

Now that you've worked Boundary Solution Step 4 by taking action to do what needs to be done, asking for help, making a request, or making the choice to do nothing, it's time to proceed to the final step of the 5-SBS: Evaluate Your Results. Hopefully, your boundary work was a success, in which case you'll celebrate! If it wasn't, you'll learn specific tools for dealing with boundaries that "didn't work," including broken agreements, and boundary violations.

CHAPTER EIGHT

Boundary Solution Step 5: Evaluate Your Results—Mission Accomplished . . . or Not: When Boundaries are Broken

"Success is not final, failure is not fatal:
it is the courage to continue that counts."

—Winston Churchill

The final step in the 5-SBS is Evaluate Your Results. Taking stock of what happened as a result of working the first four steps gives you an opportunity to celebrate, re-assess, or decide on next steps if there's been a broken agreement or boundary violation. If you don't review and evaluate the results of the action you've taken, you won't be able to determine whether it was effective or missed the mark. Hopefully, your boundary work was successful. But sometimes, even with good efforts, the process doesn't go as smoothly as you may have anticipated.

One of the most common complaints about boundary work is that a boundary was set but it "didn't work." What this usually means is that the person asked for or demanded something and didn't get it. While it goes without saying that we don't always get what we want, if you conclude that a boundary didn't work without first reviewing what happened or exploring other possible responses, you may be giving up on your wants and needs prematurely. When a boundary "doesn't work," it may mean that the original boundary wasn't as clear, measurable, or effective as it could have been. In most cases, there are almost always other actions that haven't been taken.

CELEBRATE YOUR SUCCESS!

If you followed through on an action you committed to—either something you accomplished yourself or one where you sought help—congratulations! Healing and growth occur in baby steps, and it's important to take time to honor yourself when you've followed through with an action that contributes to your safety, well-being, and growth.

If you created an agreement with your partner and the agreement has been honored—maybe not perfectly, but at least the majority of the time—congratulations! Often, when partners identify a boundary and implement it they're amazed at how easy it was and how empowered they feel. For example, say you requested a weekly check-in with the addict on Tuesday nights and the check-in has happened five of the past six weeks, on schedule. Although less than perfect, this outcome is not only a successful boundary, it's also an important building block for the repair and rehabilitation of your relationship.

Unfortunately, sometimes agreements, contracts, and boundaries are broken. As disappointing as that can be, you still have options.

WHEN YOU DON'T GET THE OUTCOME YOU WANTED

When a boundary "doesn't work" there can be a variety of reasons including lack of follow-through of the action you committed to in Step 4, unclear agreements that lack a specific, measurable outcome, or an outright boundary violation.

Obviously, if you didn't follow through with the action you committed to in Step 4, it's important for you to do some exploration within yourself about why you failed to take action. Were your plans unrealistic either in terms of time, energy, capability, or readiness? Were you fearful of the consequences of the action you committed to? Were you honestly committed to the action or the outcome? Were you highly activated or triggered when you made the plan?

For example, if your action step was to get tested for sexually transmitted infections, and you realized that you weren't ready to follow through with it, explore the reasons it was difficult for you. Perhaps you would rather not go to your family physician for testing or you're fearful of the results, or you're (justifiably) angry that you're in a situation that requires this level of self-care and self-protection. See if there are smaller, easier action steps you're confident you can do now. It's often necessary to break down tasks into smaller chunks that feel more doable.

Another reason we don't follow through on action items is that we didn't put any accountability in place. For example, if you committed to going to the doctor to get STI testing but didn't follow through, consider telling a friend, sponsor, or therapist of your intention, along with identifying a date by which you will either make the appointment or go to the doctor.

Yet another reason boundaries sometimes "don't work" is that the agreement wasn't clear. Did you want to know the addict's travel plans, but you didn't ask him to tell you within a certain time frame—forty-eight hours before his planned departure, for example? If the agreement lacked clarity or specificity, return to Boundary Solution Step 4. Revise and restate the request to create a new agreement.

THE BOUNDARY WAS BROKEN . . . WHAT NOW?

When a boundary is broken or violated, partners often give up and conclude that boundaries don't work. This is a common misconception about boundary work—believing that if we tell the other person what we want, it will be honored and that will be the end of that. It usually doesn't work that way.

Saying that boundaries don't work because they're sometimes broken is like saying that laws don't work because sometimes they're broken! The problem isn't with boundaries—as a concept. The problem lies with the clarity and quality of the agreement, as well as the ability of the participating individuals to know their limits, and uphold their promises.

When you make an agreement with the sex addict and he doesn't follow through, it can be disappointing or even devastating—depending on the severity of the issue. If the issue was a minor one that isn't significantly triggering for you, you may not have a strong reaction. On the other hand, if the agreement involves acting-out behaviors or other matters that potentially threaten your safety, jeopardize the relationship, or are deeply hurtful to you, you will need to use Boundary Solution Step 5 to determine your next steps.

The first thing you need to ask yourself is how important the issue is to you using the scale of one to ten. Doing so not only helps you quantify and clarify how important it is to you, but it also helps you decide what actions to take.

For example, let's say your partner agreed to tell you in advance if he planned to have lunch with colleagues. Then one day he came home and casually mentioned that he had lunch with several colleagues that day. Although you were disappointed, when you rated your level of upset or disappointment—a two on a scale of one to ten—it was not very important to you. Based on this number, you may choose to either ask for a repair (discussed later in this chapter) or simply do nothing, especially if your partner apologizes or demonstrates sincere remorse for his oversight.

On the other hand, if your partner broke an agreement to have no contact with a former acting-out partner, you will likely have a stronger response to this boundary violation. Your level of distress about this incident may be a nine out of ten. Clearly, your response to this broken agreement needs to reflect how important the issue is to you. For example, you wouldn't rate failure to take out the garbage as a ten, or having an affair with your best friend as a one. Once you've determined the level of importance the broken agreement has for you, you can proceed to the next step of determining how you want to respond.

Occasionally, agreements are broken due to factors outside a person's control. For example, if you requested that your partner attend three twelve-step meetings a week but weather, a car repair, or a sick child prevented that from happening, there may be no need for a repair or even a conversation.

> *"Failure is a detour, not a dead-end street."*
>
> —Zig Ziglar

YOUR OPTIONS FOR HANDLING BROKEN AGREEMENTS AND BOUNDARY VIOLATIONS

When a boundary is broken or violated, there are four possible responses, depending on the importance of the issue, your ability to create the outcome without making a request, and whether the issue is a long or short-term problem.

Here are the four possible responses to a boundary violation:

1. Return to Boundary Solution Step 4 and repeat the request and/or request a repair or an amends from the other person.

2. Return to Boundary Solution Step 4 and take necessary action, if possible, to create the result you want—or get your needs met—without the participation of the other person.

3. Return to Boundary Solution Step 1 and work Steps 1–4 based on the new issue.

4. Do nothing and accept powerlessness (provided you can let go without believing you're a victim).

1. Return to Step 4 and repeat the request and/or request a repair or an amends from the other person.

In the example where the addict didn't tell his partner in advance that he was going to lunch with colleagues, the partner could simply restate the request and re-establish the agreement.

A second option that can either stand alone or be paired with a reconfirmation of the agreement is a repair. A repair, in the context of boundary work, is an action requested from or offered by a person who violates a boundary. Repairs are amends or "apologies through action." They can take many forms depending on the seriousness of the boundary violation. They're sometimes referred to as acts of contrition—an amends for an offense.

An example of a simple repair would be if you asked your partner to pick up bread on the way home from work and he forgot, even though he agreed to do it. When he gets home and realizes he forgot the bread, he could offer a repair by immediately leaving to go to the store, or committing to get the bread before it's needed.

Here is an example of how a discussion about repair between the partner and addict might sound. The partner in this example is using the Talking Format (see Appendix):

Partner: "I was looking at our bank statement today and saw that you took out $200 from the ATM. We had an agreement that you would only take out $100 (data). When I saw that you had taken out $200 I thought you didn't care about our agreement (thought). I felt angry and afraid (emotions)."

Addict: "You're right, we did have an agreement and I'm sorry I took out more cash than we agreed on. It makes sense to me that you feel angry and scared. I had a doctor's appointment that day and didn't have a checkbook with me so I withdrew the cash to pay the doctor. I will get the receipt right now and bring it to you. If something like that happens again I will call and discuss it with you first. Is there anything else you would like from me?"

As repairs go, this one is near perfect because it includes the following components:

- Addict led with agreement when he said, "You're right, we did have an agreement . . . "

- Validation of the partner's feelings when the addict says, "It makes sense to me that you would feel . . . "

- Immediate accountability—offering "evidence" by providing the receipt.

- Information about how the incident happened and an explanation about how the money was spent.

- An offer by the person who broke the agreement (addict) to do it differently in the future.

- An invitation to the partner to see if there is something else she would like from the addict.

If appropriate, the partner could have included a request at the end of her original statement. The request might be to provide receipts for the cash spent. If the agreement has been broken before, the partner may want to renegotiate the agreement and request another arrangement that will ensure that a similar incident won't happen again. For example, the partner could request that they go to the bank together twice a month to withdraw cash, and that the addict not withdraw cash alone for a specified period of time.

Repairs may also be used for more serious issues. An example of a higher-level repair might be financial restitution by the sex addict for being deceptive with money, bank accounts, and/or spending the couples' money on sexual acting out. A financial restitution repair could involve the addict giving his partner money—equal to the amount he spent on acting out (which could include interest)—to place in a separate, individual bank account to be used in any way the partner wishes. Other higher-level repairs include moving to a new home (or even another city) due to the addict acting out with affair partners in the couple's primary residence, selling a vehicle that was part of the addict's acting-out rituals or behaviors, or changing jobs due to ongoing, regular contact with a coworker who is also a former affair partner.

2. Return to Step 4 and take necessary action, if possible, to create the result you want—or get your needs met—without the participation of the other person.

A second potential response to a boundary violation is to create the result you want without the participation or cooperation of the other person. Depending on the issue, this may or may not be possible.

For example, if you requested the sex addict to attend meetings and he didn't follow through, you don't have the power to make that happen. On the other hand, if the addict said he would install filtering software on the computer because of your concerns about how your children may be unintentionally exposed to his past online activities and he didn't follow through, you can—and likely should—take the action to create this outcome yourself.

If you choose to create the outcome yourself after a broken agreement, it's extremely important to ask yourself whether or not you can take the necessary action without thinking you're a victim. If you will, you need to either re-establish the agreement (perhaps with more clarity and accountability in the form of deadlines, for example) or you need to spend some time exploring how you might accomplish what you want without making yourself a victim of your own mindset.

If you struggle with understanding the difference between being a victim and taking care of yourself, Marshall Rosenberg, author of *Nonviolent Communication*, offers a simple exercise to replace victim thinking with a more empowered mindset. He recommends that when you notice yourself saying, "I *have to* _____," replace the "have to" with "choose to," by identifying the personal need you're fulfilling for yourself by choosing a particular course of action.

Using the example above about installing filtering software, you will make yourself a victim if you tell yourself "I have to install filtering software on the computer because he didn't do it." To make the shift from, "I have to" to "I choose to," ask yourself: "What need am I fulfilling by making the choice to _____ (in this case, install the software)?" The need you're fulfilling by installing the software could be for safety, protection of your children, peace of mind, a sense of competence, or simply to eliminate something from your to do list!

After replacing "have to" with "choose to," the new statement would be, "I choose to install filtering software on the computer because I need peace of mind knowing that my children are safe when they use the home computer."

If you decide to create the outcome for yourself rather than reestablishing or renegotiating the agreement with the addict, I urge you to complete this simple exercise to help you avoid resentments and victim thinking.

3. Return to Step 1 and work Steps 1–4 based on the new issue.

There are times when reestablishing, renegotiating, or creating the outcome you want through your own actions simply isn't possible. Perhaps you're dealing with a repeated broken agreement or you've experienced a significant impact from a boundary violation. In cases like this, you must increase your level of self-care around getting your needs met. In boundary work, this is the step where partners are most vulnerable to giving up, or in more extreme cases leaving the relationship, because they don't know what to do next.

What does it mean to increase your level of self-care? Boundary work—at its core—is about self-care and self-protection. By drawing limits with yourself and others, you take care of yourself. When someone breaks an agreement with you or violates your boundaries in a significant way, a natural and healthy instinct is to create safety and protection.

If you have an agreement with the sex addict that he won't have contact with any former acting-out partners, imagine how you would feel if he broke the agreement. You would feel angry, sad, and fearful. When you're with the sex addict, you may notice that your anger increases or that you don't want to be physically close to him or touch him. This is a normal and natural response to fully experiencing the emotion of anger. If you're paying attention to your thoughts and emotions, you may choose to limit contact or even sleep in a separate room for a period of time.

As mentioned earlier, when choosing how to handle a broken agreement or boundary violation, your response must match or be proportional to the boundary violation. If you asked the addict to comply with his therapist's recommendations around how many twelve-step meetings he should go to each week, and he went to one less meeting than the therapist recommended, divorce would not be a proportional response. In that case, you might merely express your feelings and let your partner know how his lack of follow-through with recovery impacts you and the way you feel about the relationship. However, when the issue involves a more significant breach—the addict having contact with a former affair partner or lying about his whereabouts—a low level response such as simply telling him how you feel, or worse—doing nothing—isn't advisable.

PARTNERS SPEAK

"I didn't realize until after the relationship was over how often he had violated my boundaries over the years. He constantly shamed and belittled me and asked me to do things sexually that made me uncomfortable and that I really didn't want to do. Looking back I see that not only did he violate my boundaries but I also violated my own boundaries doing things that aren't what I believe in.

"I worry about getting into another relationship in the future. I worry that I'll let my partner treat me the way he did. I'm working hard on myself, doing trauma work to heal what happened in my relationship with the addict and even deeper work from my family growing up where all this got started for me. I don't think I would have put up with as much from the addict if I had been treated with more respect and love when I was younger. I'm determined not to let it happen again."

—Anonymous

If you've arrived here at Step 5 and you're facing a broken agreement that is significant for you, you need to return to Boundary Solution Step 1 and work the first four Steps based on the new reality—the broken agreement or boundary violation. The data for Step 1 are the details of boundary violation, along with your thoughts and emotions about the data.

Work through the first three steps of the 5-SBS based on the new issue: 1) Identify Your Reality, 2) Identify Your Needs and Create Your Vision, and 3) Identify Your Power Center. When you get to Step 4, if you choose to take action you must keep in mind that you're dealing with a boundary violation when deciding what to do. A simple request is not an option because the request you previously made wasn't honored. For example, if you had an agreement with the sex addict that he wouldn't contact former acting-out partners and he has repeatedly broken the agreement, the action you choose should not be to request (again) that he not contact any acting-out partners. This would be a classic example of doing the same thing repeatedly while hoping for a different outcome—insanity.

> When boundaries are broken, especially
> repeatedly, you must increase your level of
> self-care by taking actions that have a higher
> probability of getting your needs met, or
> creating the protection you need to avoid
> further boundary violations.

In the example where the addict had contact with a former acting-out partner, there are several options to increase your level of self-care:

- Limit contact with the addict while you sort through your next steps (limiting contact could include sleeping in a separate bedroom, reducing social or family-oriented contact, or living temporarily with a friend or relative).

- Separate from the addict for a designated period of time.

- Tell the addict that if he has contact with a former acting-out partner again you will ask for a therapeutic separation (only if you are 100 percent certain you will follow through with this consequence, and if it's not motivated by revenge or retaliation).

SELF-CARE, CONSEQUENCES, AND PUNISHMENT

Responding to significant boundary violations or repeated broken agreements is the area of boundary work where partners often fail to create effective solutions because they—and addicts—confuse self-care with consequences and punishment.

CONSEQUENCE

A result or effect of an action or condition.

PUNISHMENT

The infliction or imposition of a penalty as retribution for an offense.

In doing the self-care of boundary work, consequences are a natural result of the addict's choices and behavior. Consequences in boundary work are not something done to the addict by the partner. They are not punishment. This distinction is important and must be understood as you face situations where you need to increase your self-care in order to address boundary violations.

If you're angry with the addict—so much so that you're uncomfortable interacting socially or sleeping in the same bed with him—your choice to distance from or eliminate contact is clearly an act of self-care for you. You simply feel better having less contact, given the circumstances. The addict may experience your self-care (boundary) as a consequence of his behavior. However, the boundary is *not* a punishment as defined above.

Of course, partners do sometimes attempt to punish the addict or use boundaries as a weapon. In fact, sometimes it's impossible to tell the difference between good boundary work and punishment. The communication of the boundary to the addict, and the spirit in which it is carried out, will determine whether the partner is practicing boundary work or "power over," in the form of a punishment. The fundamental difference between boundary work as self-care and punishment is in the intention. When it's punishment disguised as a boundary, you can usually spot it in the follow-through (or lack thereof).

For example, if you decide that you want to sleep separately from the addict because of repeated broken agreements or boundary violations, and you prefer that he sleep in another bedroom, you can request that he do so. If he says no to your request and instead of taking action by sleeping in the other bedroom yourself, you remain in the same bedroom with him and complain that he didn't do what you asked him to do, you have made yourself a victim, engaged in a power struggle with the addict, and weren't practicing solid boundary work when you made the request.

> Effective and healthy boundary work
> means you're willing to take action to get
> your needs met, even when the addict
> says no to your request.

COMMIT—WITH CONFIDENCE—TO YOUR CONSEQUENCE

When deciding what action to take for boundary violations, you must be 100 percent confident that you will follow through with future boundaries you express to the addict. For example, with one of the possible responses given above—"Tell the addict that if he has contact with a former acting-out partner again you will separate from the addict"—you must be absolutely sure you will follow through before you communicate the boundary to the addict.

If you express a boundary and don't follow through, your boundaries are merely idle threats that cause you to lose credibility. Sadly, you not only lose credibility with the person to whom you express the boundary, but also with yourself. As a partner of an addict, you have experienced profound violations of trust. It is far better for you to delay expressing a boundary to the addict than to create one, not follow through, and then become untrustworthy to yourself.

When you set boundaries, the addict may attempt to manipulate you into changing your mind by calling you selfish, saying you're punishing, controlling, or telling him what to do. If you feel confused or begin to second-guess your choices, discuss it with a trusted person. Are you feeling grounded and centered? Do you feel happier and calmer when you're acting on the boundaries you set? If you are, your boundaries are appropriate and healthy. The pushback you're getting—in the form of accusations or even attacks—is an attempt to get you to change your mind or go back to the status quo. Remind yourself that most people will not applaud your change of behavior when you begin doing boundary work. As uncomfortable as it is, one of the ways you'll know you're on the right track is that the people in your life with whom you're setting boundaries aren't usually happy about it. That's why it's important to have the support of trusted friends, a sponsor, or therapist to reach out to for help when you're feeling confused or unsure.

Partners sometimes ignore or override their instincts due to beliefs about what they should or shouldn't do, or because they struggle to honor and act on their reality. For example, you may have a belief you must behave in certain ways because you're married to the addict (have sex, sleep in the same bed, or attend social functions together, for example). You may feel distrustful about the addict's honesty about his recovery, yet choose to have unprotected sex with him. Or, as in the example above, you may be furious with the addict because he had lunch with a former affair partner, yet you choose to sleep in the same bed with him. When your emotions don't match your actions and choices, it's time to do some serious exploration about why you're choosing not to honor and act on your reality.

4. Do nothing and accept powerlessness (provided you can let go without having a resentment).

When you get to the fourth and final option for handling boundary violations, you have accepted that you're powerless to create the result you want. You may have experienced repeated boundary violations and/or broken agreements. You may have tried all possible solutions and they've been unsuccessful. It's time to accept powerlessness.

However, before you let go, be sure to examine your choice by using the one-to-ten rating system to determine how important the issue is to you. If you rate the issue as a ten (ongoing infidelity or dishonesty, for instance), and you want to make the choice to do nothing, what you're saying in effect is that you're accepting a situation that causes you great distress. You have a right to your own choices, including the choice to stay in a relationship with someone who is chronically unfaithful. However, if doing so causes you a high level of distress and pain, the choice to do nothing should ring some very loud alarm bells for you.

If you choose to do nothing and accept powerlessness, you can't later say that you're a victim of the same behaviors around which you've chosen not to do boundary work or practice self-care. If you live in a neighborhood where thieves regularly take valuables out of your car because you don't lock your car door, your choice to leave your door unlocked contributes to your repeated victimization. In the same way, if you choose not to do boundary work when it's warranted, you're responsible for not protecting yourself.

Accepting powerlessness shouldn't be a result of sticking your head in the sand, avoiding conflict, or failing to own your power and simply giving up. Rather, it should be the end result of having considered all possible options and making a conscious, empowered, and informed choice not to act. As we discussed in Chapter Six (Identify Your Power Center), accepting powerlessness is not a passive choice. It's an action in its own right and can be an opportunity to connect with your Higher Power. Through prayer and conscious contact, you can release the problem to a power greater than yourself knowing that the outcome is in the hands of God, the Universe, the Divine, or however you conceive of your Higher Power.

Go ahead now and complete the exercise at the end of this chapter on the "5-SBS Clarifier" you downloaded. If your situation warrants returning to the prior steps due to broken agreements or boundary violations, work Steps 1–4 again.

You now have all the information you need to work the 5-SBS! These steps can be used for any situation in which you need to do boundary work with yourself, the addict, or anyone else in your life.

Although they're simple, these steps aren't always easy. Partners who struggle with valuing themselves or have other challenges such as preexisting trauma may experience difficulty completing all, or some, of these steps. In the next chapter we'll look at some of the roadblocks and barriers to practicing effective boundary work, along with solutions to these challenges.

▄ EXERCISE

BOUNDARY SOLUTION STEP 5: EVALUATE YOUR RESULTS

If your boundary work was successful, congratulations!

If the boundary missed the mark, ask yourself the following questions:

• Did I follow through on the action I committed to in Step 4? If not, recommit or re-evaluate the action.

• If I made a request, was the agreement clear? If not, return to Step 4 and revise the request.

- Was the agreement broken (boundary violation)? If yes, determine how important this issue is to you on a scale of one to ten: "This issue is a _____ for me." This number will help you determine your next steps.

For broken agreements and boundary violations, your options are as follows:

1. Return to Step 4 and repeat your request and/or request a repair or an amends from the other person.

2. Return to Step 4 and take necessary action, if possible, to create the result you want—or get your needs met—without the participation of the other person.

3. Return to Step 1 and work Steps 1–4 based on the new issue.

4. Do nothing and accept powerlessness (provided you can let go without believing you're a victim).

CHAPTER NINE

Speed Bumps, Roadblocks, and Crash Landings: Hidden Barriers to Boundary Work and What to Do About Them

PARTNERS SPEAK

"At first I thought it was all his problem and that he was the one who needed to do something about it. I thought if he got better then I would feel better. After a while I realized that wasn't true. I kept going to my therapist, his therapist, and a couples' therapist hoping that they would change him. I really thought they could.

"Things got worse and worse. After a while I just gave up. I filed for divorce. I think he was shocked. I know everything happens for a reason but I wonder how things might have turned out differently if I had learned boundaries and asked for what I wanted instead of just hoping and praying that he would be different."

—Anonymous

Even with guidance, good intentions, and a solid support system, partners sometimes fail to get clarity, own their power, and implement the boundary work they know they need to do. If unresolved issues are holding you back and sabotaging your boundary work, take heart . . . and be gentle with yourself. This is an opportunity to access the kind, loving, and understanding guide within to help you move beyond the barriers to practicing the exquisite self-care and protection you deserve.

If you're struggling to get started or take action with boundary work, it's time to dig a little deeper into the possible root causes. A good place to start is to ask yourself whether you were completely committed to the boundary you set or wanted to set. Partners sometimes react—rather than respond—by setting boundaries they're not fully committed to, especially when they're triggered or highly activated.

Maybe you told the addict you would take a therapeutic separation or leave the relationship if he relapsed again, but when that happened you didn't follow through. Or maybe you told yourself you would no longer be sexually intimate with the sex addict unless he completed a formal disclosure, yet you're still being sexual with him despite his failure to do so.

There are many reasons partners struggle to do effective boundary work, and we'll discuss the most common ones in this chapter. Recommendations for next steps are offered for partners who realize they need more individual work in a particular area before they can proceed.

As you read each section, you'll notice that many are interrelated and overlap. For example, most people who have problems with esteem will tend to overvalue their relationship or their partner, and will likely have some family of origin trauma to work through. Partners who delay following through with strong boundaries such as separation or divorce because of parenting young children typically also have financial constraints complicating their situation.

Here are the most common reasons partners have difficulty creating and maintaining effective boundaries:

- Issues of esteem and worth

- Difficulty with emotional regulation

- Family and financial considerations

- Addiction or untreated mental health concerns

- Overvaluing the relationship or the addict (love addiction)

- Trauma—family of origin and preexisting adult trauma

- Undisclosed secrets

- Situations of domestic abuse

ESTEEM AND WORTH

Because boundary work is essentially an act of self-care and self-love, if you struggle to esteem yourself you will have problems creating and setting boundaries. The truth is—whether you're aware of it or not—you're worthy right now in this very moment, just as you are. You don't have to do anything or be anything other than who you are in order to "deserve" to get your needs and wants met, or to make requests of anyone for anything.

If feeling worthy is a challenge for you, you may believe you don't deserve to have a healthy, functional relationship or to be treated with respect. You may think you're damaged goods, or not smart or attractive enough. Partners sometimes believe that no one else would want them, and because of that belief they have difficulty setting boundaries out of fear of losing the only relationship they think they'll ever have.

Esteeming oneself is experienced on a continuum from feeling less than at one end of the spectrum, to feeling better than on the other. When you see yourself as less than others or "one down," you will feel toxic shame. At the other extreme you will feel better than others or "one up." This is grandiosity, arrogance, or—at its worst—narcissism. When partners are in a state of feeling chronically one down, they have difficulty practicing self-care, speaking their truth, and getting their needs met.

In terms of boundary work, partners who feel one down may struggle to identify the outcome they want (Boundary Solution Step 2) or make requests of the addict (Boundary Solution Step 4) because they don't believe they have the right to want or ask for more. When partners go one up on the addict, they may punish him or engage in "power over" strategies as discussed in Chapter Six. They will make demands rather than requests and offend from the victim position.

When you esteem yourself, you're in the "I'm okay, you're okay" position. When you fully embody this mindset—which, by the way, is quite difficult to do—you won't believe you're better than or less than any other person. Seeing yourself as neither better than nor less than is a powerful, spiritual experience.

If you want to know more about where you stand in terms of esteeming yourself, try this simple exercise: Notice throughout the day when you feel better than or less than, or when you go one up or one down. You will be amazed at how susceptible you are—literally moment by moment—to fluctuations in the way you esteem yourself. It's true for all of us.

You can directly influence the amount of time you stay in the healthy middle between better than and less than by practicing esteem-building behaviors. Any act of self-care is an esteem-building behavior because you're treating yourself like someone who deserves your care and respect. Taking care of your basic needs such as proper nutrition, hygiene, and exercise, along with regular medical and dental care, are also esteem builders.

Begin to pay mindful attention to your internal self-talk, as well as the way others in your life talk to you, including the addict. If your self-talk is an ongoing monologue of you're not good enough, not attractive enough, not smart enough, or just plain broken or defective, you will have serious difficulty esteeming yourself. If people in your life—your partner, family members, boss, or friends—shame you for the way you think, the way you look, or what you do, work on developing a "healthy allergy" to comments, interactions, and people who shame or belittle you in any way. At best, this kind of behavior is not relational—at worst, it's abusive. These are all opportunities to practice boundaries, either by putting limits on your negative self-talk or setting boundaries with the critical, unsupportive people in your life.

DIFFICULTY WITH EMOTIONAL REGULATION

Emotional regulation problems can look identical to the post-traumatic stress responses commonly seen in partners of sex addicts both pre- and post-discovery. The difference between post-traumatic stress responses and emotional regulation issues is that the partner's emotional regulation problems existed well before discovery or disclosure, and more likely before the relationship with the addict.

Most of us struggle with emotional regulation to some extent. Emotional regulation is the ability to be aware of, reflect on, and manage your emotional responses in the service of meeting your needs, wants, or goals, and being relational with others. Individuals with emotional regulation issues have difficulty self-soothing, or calming themselves. They react rather than respond, and they tend to look toward external solutions for internal problems. For example, they believe that other people are the primary source of their pain or anger, rather than looking at the internal thought processes that are creating difficult emotions, or how they may have contributed to the problem.

In terms of boundary work, a partner who struggles with emotional regulation will consistently and impulsively (without thoughtful reflection) create boundaries in reaction to intense feelings of fear, pain, anger, or shame. She may become literally overwrought with emotion over incidents and issues that are only mildly or moderately activating (such as the sex addict being ten to fifteen minutes late coming home). She may threaten divorce over minor events or become emotionally or physically abusive when she is highly activated, fearful, or anxious. Self-soothing skills such as conscious breathing, correcting distorted thinking like "I will die without him," or placing limits on activities that are unnecessarily triggering, are difficult and sometimes unmanageable for people who struggle with emotional regulation. Dialectical Behavior Therapy (DBT) is a proven and effective treatment method for issues of emotional regulation (see Appendix for resources).

FAMILY AND FINANCIAL CONSIDERATIONS

If you're parenting children still living at home, you face special challenges in your healing, boundary work, and in the rehabilitation of your relationship with the addict. Simple conversations and interactions that most childfree couples take for granted either get delayed or simply don't happen for couples impacted by sex addiction who are also parenting young children.

Partners experience frequent frustration around needing to contain thoughts and emotions related to the addiction while in the presence of their children. While this kind of containment is necessary to protect children from age-inappropriate information or emotionally charged interactions with the addict, most partners experience ongoing pain as a result of the limited opportunity to freely express themselves. If you, as the partner, aren't aware of the impact of needing to consistently repress in this way, you may shut down altogether and give up trying to have any meaningful interactions with the addict.

When partners are parenting young children, they're usually reluctant to disrupt the relative stability of their children's lives by separating or divorcing the addict even when this is the best choice for the partner. You may shy away from boundary work because you believe your children will be devastated to lose the consistent presence of the other parent. Sadly, for the sake of the children, partners sometimes sacrifice their needs and wants without realizing they are modeling poor boundaries to their children in the form of teaching them that it's not okay to take care of and protect yourself.

You may have religious values or beliefs that admonish you to stay and salvage your marriage—no matter the cost. You may not have income of your own, or your financial resources may be insufficient to sustain yourself and your children without the support of the addict. When this is the case, partners may decide to "tough it out" until the children leave home.

If you're in a situation where you feel stuck, as if you have no options, I urge you to seek out an objective third party, such as a financial advisor, mentor, or therapist, to help you evaluate and explore your situation and to offer support, recommendations, and guidance. Partners sometimes hide behind financial considerations or parenting issues as a way to avoid making difficult choices to take care of themselves and create a more fulfilling life.

You need to ask yourself whether the addict's behavior jeopardizes the health and safety of your children. Obviously, if the sex addict has any sexual interest in children that is a non-negotiable boundary that warrants immediate protection of minor children. There are also other circumstances that require protection of children such as exposure to pornography or other sexually inappropriate material or experiences due to the addict's behavior. If you're ignoring situations or your intuition about the ways in which your children may be impacted by the addict's behavior, seek outside support immediately. Knowing that your children are being exposed to inappropriate sexual behavior or material and doing nothing is a form of neglect and covert sexual abuse.

ADDICTION OR UNTREATED MENTAL HEALTH CONCERNS

At the beginning of treatment when a therapist creates a treatment plan for a client, some issues must be addressed before proceeding to deeper work. These are sometimes referred to as Phase I issues. Phase I issues include active addictions or untreated mental health concerns.

If you have an active addiction—to alcohol or other drugs (including prescription drugs), gambling, sex, work, food, or exercise—you probably won't be able to engage in meaningful boundary work until the addiction is addressed. The primary reasons are related to esteem, the deception that goes hand-in-hand with any active addiction, as well as distorted thinking that leads to poor emotional regulation.

Untreated mental health concerns are another Phase I issue. Severe depression or anxiety, bipolar disorder, and personality disorders are some of the most common issues that must be treated before someone can do more in-depth individual or couples' work. If you believe you may have an untreated mental health concern, make an appointment with a qualified, board-certified psychiatrist for a comprehensive evaluation (see Appendix for resources).

OVERVALUING THE RELATIONSHIP OR THE ADDICT (LOVE ADDICTION)

Overvaluing a relationship or your partner is closely related to the issue of self-esteem. If you see the addict (or any person with whom you're in a relationship) as having more value than you, you are vulnerable to putting your needs and wants last, or worse, being exploited by the other person. Taken to an extreme, the person who overvalues his or her partner suffers from love addiction, a term Pia Mellody coined in her book *Facing Love Addiction*.

As we touched on in Chapter Six, love addiction is a serious form of codependency where one person places such a high value on another (partner, friend, family member, etc.) that the relationship becomes all-consuming, and the primary focus of the love addict's attention. When partners of sex addicts suffer from love addiction, they spend inordinate amounts of time obsessing, ruminating, and seeking information about the sex addict's activities. They may even demand to know all of the addict's thoughts and fantasies. When love addiction is severe, the love-addicted person may monitor, follow, harass, or even stalk the object of his or her obsession. The main female character in the movie *Fatal Attraction*, Alex, is an extreme example of a love-addicted person. With the widespread availability of portable electronic devices, apps, and software, it is possible to track someone without his or her knowledge twenty-four hours a day.

Most love addicts come from dysfunctional and/or addictive family systems where their emotional needs weren't met. They usually experienced emotional neglect and abandonment by one or both parents. Abandonment creates intense anxiety in children because they depend on their caretakers for their very survival. The anxiety created by neglect and abandonment is carried forward into adulthood until recovery or other intensive healing work is done. This anxiety—felt internally as a very young and vulnerable part of themselves—is one of the reasons love addicted individuals will often feel as though their survival is dependent on having or being with the object of their addiction.

If you want to know whether you struggle with love addiction, consider taking the Love Addiction Test in the Appendix. Twelve-step groups such as Sex & Love Addicts Anonymous (SLAA), Co-Dependents Anonymous (CODA), or Love Addicts Anonymous (LAA) can be helpful resources for anyone impacted by love addiction. (The Appendix includes a complete list of twelve-step organizations.)

FAMILY OF ORIGIN AND PREEXISTING ADULT TRAUMA

Partners with unresolved family of origin or adult trauma that predated the discovery of the addiction often have challenges to doing effective boundary work. Your trauma history impacts how you process and navigate through discovery, disclosure, and beyond. Your responses throughout your healing journey are largely determined by your innate temperament (whether you are extroverted or introverted, or more or less expressive in your communication style, for example), and your trauma history.

Dysfunctional family systems with any of the following characteristics make us vulnerable to boundary problems in adulthood:

- Neglect and abandonment

- Family secrets

- Frequent shaming or being the family "scapegoat"

- A parent or other relative who was an addict or offender

- Regular episodes of physical abuse or witnessing the abuse of a parent or sibling

- Sexual abuse (including being exposed to age-inappropriate sexual material, conversations, or behavior)

- Lack of healthy, appropriate boundaries

Young children experience most of what happens in their family as normal even when it's severely dysfunctional or even abusive. We are literally calibrated by our family of origin—meaning we must adapt and attune ourselves to our family's dynamics in order to survive. These childhood experiences shape us in profound ways and influence the people with whom we feel comfortable, and attract to us, in adulthood.

If one or more of your family members repeatedly violated boundaries and wasn't held accountable for his or her behavior, you may believe there are certain people with whom you don't have a right to set boundaries. When an adult doesn't take responsibility for the impact of his or her behavior on others, he or she is acting above the law—assuming the position of a Higher Power or a God/ Goddess. This kind of boundary-less behavior is a toxic legacy that teaches children that some people don't have to play by the rules. Unfortunately, children who grow up in a boundary-less family system are vulnerable to exploitation and/or may become offensive to others and violate others' boundaries.

If you grew up in a family where you couldn't count on your basic needs being met, especially emotional needs, you will come to experience not getting your needs met as "the norm." If neglect was the primary form of abuse you experienced in childhood, you may feel unworthy and ask for very little, or nothing, in terms of repair and trust-building behaviors from the sex addict. You may appear somewhat neutral when receiving painful disclosure information, or regularly disengage from the addict to process your feelings alone. Female partners who come from families where women were expected to be subservient to men may struggle to use their voice and claim their rights in the relationship.

On the other hand, if you grew up in a family where the abuse was more overt (physical or sexual abuse, for example), you will be more likely to engage in control, manipulation, or "power over" strategies to get your needs met in the relationship. If your family of origin was chaotic and violent, you may lash out, yell, scream, rage, or even become physically abusive when you learn of the addict's past behaviors, slips, or relapses.

In terms of boundaries, the partner who rages or becomes abusive needs more emotional containment (restraint), whereas the partner who appears more shut down needs to be encouraged to have her feelings and express them.

If you believe experiences of your family of origin or other childhood traumas have contributed to difficulties with boundaries or other challenges in your life, seek professional help to get more information. The Appendix includes a brief questionnaire to help you identify potential areas of abuse and trauma titled, "Adverse Childhood Experiences (ACEs)." The ACEs questionnaire is based on one of the largest studies of its kind, involving more than 17,000 participants. The questionnaire is designed to assess the relationship between childhood abuse and future adult physical and mental health. Higher ACEs scores are directly related to risk factors in adulthood including depression, anxiety, heart disease, Post-Traumatic Stress Disorder, addiction, and inability to maintain intimate relationships.[5]

PARTNERS SPEAK

"My father had all the power in our house growing up. He was a rager and an offender. My mother never stood up to him and I thought of her as weak and incompetent. I think somewhere along the way I decided that it was better to be like him than like her.

"In the first few months after I found out my partner was a sex addict, I raged, threw things, punched holes in walls, and told him what to do and when to do it. I thought I had a right to treat him like that because he had cheated on me.

"It took a while in therapy for me to understand that my behavior was abusive and that no matter what had happened to me I didn't have a right to abuse anyone—not even the addict. I finally made the connection that I had chosen my dad's form of power because it felt better than being the weakling I saw my mom as. Today, power feels very different to me.

---

[5] Centers for Disease Control and Prevention: Injury Prevention & Control. "Child Maltreatment: Consequences" (January 14, 2014), www.cdc.gov/violenceprevention/childmaltreatment/consequences.html (Accessed September 12, 2015).

*Today, power means speaking my truth, setting limits
(including with myself), and being strong and clear
without being offensive or abusive."*

—Anonymous

If you have unresolved family of origin issues, I highly recommend seeking out a therapist specifically focused on resolving family of origin trauma. Many of the partners who've attended my four-day family of origin intensive *Reclaiming Wholeness*, report the following powerful results:

- Feelings of relief and overall decrease in levels of shame

- Better boundaries

- Complete reframing of how they see their childhood

- More ease in navigating through their healing process with the sex addict

- Better parenting skills and more connection to their children (including adult children)

Some partners have preexisting adult trauma that negatively impacts their ability to engage in effective boundary work. Examples of preexisting adult trauma include sexual assault, being the victim of a violent crime, or a history of physically or sexually abusive relationships. If you have untreated adult trauma, seek out a practitioner trained in trauma treatment such as Somatic Experiencing (SE), Eye Movement Desensitization and Reprocessing (EMDR), or Sensorimotor Psychotherapy. See the Appendix for further trauma resources.

SECRETS

Although the addict is typically the person in the relationship holding secrets, sometimes partners have secrets as well. Secrets include information or knowledge a partner keeps from herself through denial or unwillingness to face painful facts that would disrupt or completely alter her current life. For example, sometimes partners aren't willing to acknowledge the extent to which financial considerations keep them in the current relationship. They may have made a bargain (conscious or unconscious) with themselves to tolerate the ongoing consequences of addiction in order to maintain their lifestyle or their status in the community.

When people are holding secrets or are out of integrity—meaning they're not living in alignment with their values or aren't being the kind of person they aspire to be—they typically aren't able to set and maintain boundaries. They may believe they don't have a right to hold other people accountable because of their own faults or deceptions. Sadly, one of the hidden consequences of addiction is that addicts fail to hold others accountable for inappropriate or abusive behavior—even their children—because they don't believe they have the right. One of the milestones and markers of progress in an addict's recovery is when he begins to hold other people accountable for bad behavior. The bottom line is that it's much easier to practice boundaries when you're in integrity and in alignment with your values.

If you're holding a secret, the best course of action is to talk to a trusted person and share your secret with him or her, and then with anyone else with whom you need to disclose or make amends. Although momentarily painful, disclosing secrets reaps long-term rewards. It's an exercise in reducing shame and building esteem, and will make your boundary work easier.

SITUATIONS OF DOMESTIC ABUSE

Lastly, there are some situations, albeit rare, when a partner may truly not have the power to change her situation. Her partner may be controlling to the point that she is cut off from all support from her family, community, church, etc.—essentially a battered woman's situation. If this applies to you, you need to create a safety plan and identify two to three organizations that can help you, including a shelter if there is one available in your area. Most shelters have a twenty-four-hour hotline and often provide transportation to the shelter. They are typically safe, confidential, and have good policies in place to ensure that you will be well protected. For more resources on domestic violence see the Appendix.

Partners often discover somewhere along their healing journey that they have unresolved or unaddressed issues that surface post-discovery and disclosure. If you're facing any of the issues discussed in this chapter, I urge you to seek more information and guidance from a qualified professional or other appropriate resource.

CHAPTER TEN

Burning is Learning: How Your New Boundary Muscle Will Keep You Strong and Serene for a Lifetime

PARTNERS SPEAK

"When I began recovery I had been married for eighteen years. We did recovery together for two years. Around that time I became aware that I was not happy in the current situation. When he said he wanted a divorce, I knew in my heart I did not want to be in this marriage anymore. It has now been ten years and I choose to live my life fully, wholly, authentically, mindfully, lovingly, happily. And I continue in my recovery."

—Paula R.

One of the secrets of the 5-SBS I've saved until now—and one you've probably figured out—is that these steps aren't just for boundaries in relationships with sex addicts. Now that you're armed with these tools and information, you can use them in a variety of situations and with a variety of people in your life. Once you've mastered boundary work in the most intimate and high-stakes relationship in your life—with the addict—you'll find it's much easier to practice in relationships with less complex emotional attachments and commitments.

As with any new skill, when you begin using boundaries more consciously in your everyday life, it can initially feel awkward and stilted. There will be false starts, bumps, and blunders along the way. Just like when you learn to walk, you will fall down—and get back up—many times before you master it. And with enough practice, you become more confident in your ability to walk and, eventually, you run!

As you're learning how to create, set, and maintain boundaries, you may come across to others as a little unsure of yourself, or perhaps even aggressive. You may say to the addict, "You have to _____, it's my boundary," or "If you ever slip, I'll leave you." You may make threats in the heat of the moment that you realize later you would never act on. Or, you may wish you had created a boundary in a situation where it was fully warranted or even essential. These are all part of the learning process. Be gentle with yourself and know that, just like learning to walk, if you continue to get back up, eventually the process will be easier and more fluid.

Practicing boundaries will help you re-establish trust in yourself and your intuition. You'll begin acting on and protecting yourself because you've learned how to honor your own reality and intuition. You'll begin to spot potential boundary problems more quickly. You'll notice when something doesn't seem quite right where, in the past, you ignored your intuitive hunch. This kind of awareness will save you time, energy, and heartache.

With your newfound boundary skills, you won't need to spend as much energy on situations and people that used to take up too much of your time or that you once became unnecessarily obsessed over. You will move through difficult or conflict-laden situations with friends, family, or in the workplace with greater clarity and ease. "No" will come much easier to you. When boundaries are practiced and honed, most people find they develop a healthy aversion to drama and chaos—two of the biggest time-wasters there are.

Partners often find when they shift the focus to their own self-care and begin doing boundary work, they have a tremendous amount of untapped energy and inner resources that had been consumed by monitoring the addict's activities, obsessing over, or attempting to control people or situations over which they had no control. Boundaries free up more energy for you, your interests, your vision for your future, and all the things you may have neglected because you've been preoccupied with the sex addict and the impact of addiction on your life.

PARTNERS SPEAK

"My sex addict partner and I were enmeshed, but neither of us had any awareness of it. I didn't know where he ended and I started. When I realized how enmeshed we were, it didn't work for me anymore. When I began to detach and set boundaries, I found that I could make healthy choices for myself and learn what my needs and wants were—both in and out of the relationship. I got in touch with my loving and respectful spirit, which had been buried under all the anger and trauma from the relationship. This was very powerful to me. It allowed me to become more authentic, both with myself and with others."

—Kay

If you have children—still at home or adult children—they will benefit and learn from the way you model good boundaries. One of the greatest gifts you can give your children is the healing and recovery work you do. Your work benefits not only you, but your immediate and extended family, and future generations as well.

Children crave structure, and they thrive in environments where there is a healthy balance between freedom to be who they are, and limits to behaving in ways that aren't relational or are unsafe. If you're parenting young children still living at home, you can use what you've learned from the 5-SBS as you create boundaries for your children. The mechanics of the model are somewhat different as they apply to adult/child relationships, but many of the concepts are directly applicable to boundary work with children.

As you model healthy boundaries you're also teaching your children that they have permission to set boundaries with others and say no. Of course, there are some things children must do, and as a parent you can insist that your children do what they need to do to be safe and to keep their bodies healthy. However, there are many situations in which children have a right to say no, including when others want to physically touch them. Except in situations involving medical care or physical hygiene, children have a right to say no to any physical touch from anyone. If we, as parents, insist that our children hug Aunt Sue or Grandpa Joe every time the relative (or friend) wants a hug, we're unintentionally communicating to them that they don't have a right to say no. This sets our children up for abuse and exploitation by people who would cause them harm.

Of course the process of implementing better boundaries is not always smooth sailing. When you start practicing boundaries, people in your life—especially the addict—probably won't like it. They may call you selfish, rigid, or even a "bitch." The pushback you get may cause you to wonder whether you've done the right thing. But remember that a negative response to boundaries and limits means, at a minimum, that you're doing something different! More likely than not you're on the right track. Change is difficult for individuals and relationships. Although you may find it challenging to stick to your boundary in the face of pushback, negativity, or outright hostility, remember that it's essential for your long-term health and well-being.

As you apply the principles and the steps of the 5-SBS in all your relationships, you'll move through difficult situations with more ease and grace, enjoying the clarity and serenity that come from the practice of good boundary work.

CHAPTER ELEVEN

Partners Beyond Betrayal: Trust, Gratitude, and Forgiveness

"Freedom is what you do with
what's been done to you."

—Jean-Paul Sartre

Having lived through deceit, betrayal, and even abuse, you may find the ideas and concepts in this chapter—trust, gratitude, and forgiveness—difficult, or even infuriating, to read about. Perhaps you are filled with so much despair that these words sound like a foreign, painful language, or worse, an assault. Honor where you are today, and if you're feeling even a tiny bit receptive to exploring what's here, I hope you will. As the slogan says, "Take what you like and leave the rest."

PARTNERS SPEAK

"My own healing was the gift I found in recovery. I am grateful for the work I've done. I never imagined when I started doing the hard, painful work what a rich, full life I would find. I found a large piece of my own wounding from childhood that had been hidden from my conscious awareness until then. Forgiveness grew slowly, leaving room for love and happiness in my marriage. I created a life with boundaries— learning to trust myself, and then my husband."

—Gayle

Depending on where you are in your journey, it may be difficult—or even impossible—to imagine that you will ever be a "partner beyond betrayal." I hope to inspire you to adopt another mindset. If you stay true to yourself and your own healing work, you will come to know that while you were betrayed in the past, you are not a victim today. If you've managed to make it this far, I know you're committed to creating a serene, joyful, and empowered life—with or without the sex addict. You deserve all of that, and it is completely achievable for you.

WILL I EVER TRUST AGAIN?

If you've been wondering whether you'll ever be able to trust again, the simple answer is "yes." However, you'll likely never trust again the way you did pre-discovery, and that is not necessarily a bad thing. The difference between pre-discovery trust and post-discovery trust is that the source of trust post-discovery is based on the quality of your self-care, your ability to trust your intuition and inner knowing, as well as on paying more attention to the sex addict's behaviors and actions rather than his words.

There's an intangible quality about the way addicts who are genuinely working a recovery program show up. It's a kind of "you'll know it when you see it" experience. When partners are reeling from the trauma of discovery and disclosure, this vague and indefinable assurance is understandably met with strong doubt and suspicion. I fully appreciate and respect the sentiment.

Here are eight signs indicating that the sex addict is either becoming or is, in fact, more trustworthy:

1. He is fully engaged in recovery activities without expressing resentment or acting as though he feels like a victim.

2. When you ask questions about the past or his recovery work, he's open to answering your questions and only occasionally defensive.

3. When you're together as a couple you feel that he is fully present most of the time.

4. He is transparent and forthcoming about his whereabouts, use of money, and his online or electronic activities.

5. He demonstrates the ability to empathize with your feelings, especially about his past behaviors.

6. When you express discomfort about an event, activity, or even an article of his clothing that is a trigger for you, he is open to making changes in an effort to repair damage caused in the past.

7. When you make reasonable requests, he either agrees or negotiates a mutually agreeable solution.

8. In general, he appears more engaged in life with less forgetfulness and distraction.

In addition, if the use of polygraph exams is part of your relationship's trust-building path, they can provide verification of the addict's honesty and trustworthiness.

As you heal, you will regain trust in your intuition and your ability to take care of yourself whether the addict stays in recovery or not. Once you know—in the deepest part of your being—that you will be okay no matter what happens, your need to verify and have a guarantee of the trustworthiness of others, including the addict, will diminish.

GRATITUDE

PARTNERS SPEAK

"I am grateful for recovery. When I started in recovery, I was doing it to help my addict and I was very resentful. I thought, he is the one with the problem, why should I have to attend meetings? The first time I heard another woman in a meeting say she was grateful for recovery, I thought, she must be smoking something!"

—Kay

Smoking something indeed! The idea of a "grateful partner of a sex addict" may seem ludicrous. How can a partner feel gratitude for all the pain and trauma she has gone through as a result of being in a relationship with a sex addict? Remarkably, many partners reach a point in their healing and recovery when they realize they would have never experienced the gifts, growth, or the empowerment they acquired without the unwelcome trauma—addiction—that came into their life.

It is a basic fact of human nature that we rarely grow without struggle, pain, fear, or conflict. And while no one would ever wish the kind of devastation partners experience on anyone, ultimately what we do with what happens to us is more important than what happens to us.

The impact of sex addiction inspires and pushes many a partner to:

- Pursue a career that she had always dreamed of but thought was out of reach;

- Take care of herself physically and emotionally in ways that eluded her pre-discovery;

- Return to school to get a long-wanted degree, certification, or new skill set;

- Establish her independence and assertiveness in the relationship, where before she yielded too much responsibility and power to the addict around finances, or other important decisions;

- Explore or rekindle her own sexuality and experience greater sexual fulfillment.

If the concept of gratitude feels utterly impossible for you, or if you find yourself feeling particularly discouraged, or stuck in a victim mindset, spend some time reading or listening to the stories of people who have overcome enormous odds to live an abundant and successful life. Viktor Frankl and Nelson Mandela are some great examples. Here are a few more:

- Beckie Brown. Beckie founded the first chapter of Mothers Against Drunk Driving (MADD) in Pasco County, FL in 1980 after her eighteen-year-old son, Marcus, was killed in an accident involving a nineteen-year-old drunk driver.[6]

- Zainab Salbi. Zainab is an Iraqi-American author and women's rights activist. Born in Iraq, her father was Saddam Hussein's personal pilot. In an effort to protect Zainab from Hussein, her mother sent her to the United States

---

[6] "History of MADD," Mothers Against Drunk Drivers, accessed December 22, 2015, http://www.madd.org/about-us/mission/.

at the age of twenty in an arranged marriage to a man who sexually abused her. At the time, Zainab felt deeply betrayed by her mother and didn't learn until much later her mother's reasons for sending her to the United States. After escaping her abusive marriage, she founded Women for Women International in 1993 at the age of twenty-three. Today, Women for Women International has helped more than 400,000 women in eight countries around the world affected by war and conflict.[7]

• Amy Purdy. Amy survived Meningococcal Meningitis at nineteen years old, and went on to become a para-athlete snowboarder, founder of Adaptive Action Sports, and competed in Dancing with the Stars in 2014 despite having two prosthetic legs.[8]

• Katie Piper. Katie is a former model from the United Kingdom who survived having acid thrown in her face by a man who was solicited by Katie's boyfriend to carry out the outrageous crime. Not only was her face disfigured in the attack, but she also lost her eyesight. She founded the Katie Piper Foundation, a nonprofit organization to raise awareness of the plight of victims of burns and disfigurement injuries. A documentary was produced about her experience titled *Katie: My Beautiful Face*.[9]

There are many other examples of people who endured horrendous traumatic events and went on to surpass the achievements and successes of their pre-trauma self. Let their stories offer you hope and inspire you to envision a future that is beyond what may seem possible at the moment.

---

[7] "About Us," Women for Women International's website, accessed January 10, 2016, http://www.womenforwomen.org/about-us,

[8] "Amy's Story," Amy Purdy's website, accessed December 22, 2015, http://amypurdy.com/about/.

[9] "Meet Katie," website of The Katie Piper Foundation, accessed December 22, 2015, http://katiepiperfoundation.org.uk/meet-katie/.

FORGIVENESS

*"Genuine forgiveness does not deny anger
but faces it head-on."*

—Alice Miller

Forgiveness is a delicate topic that creates confusion, pain, and even guilt for partners who've been betrayed and traumatized by the addict in their life. Partners sometimes deeply desire to forgive, but get frustrated with themselves because they can't do it. This kind of inner turmoil and conflict can slow down a partner's healing process because she's not allowing her emotions to flow freely—including anger.

Forgiveness is a process. It's not something you can make happen. Forgiveness is very organic, and like all organic processes you can't force it to happen.

Imagine a tiny seed buried in soil where you can't see it yet. You're not sure it's there, but little by little it's preparing to sprout. When the small seedling sprouts, it will be a fragile, tender stalk. This is a time when you might put protection around it to give it a chance to get stronger before exposing it to the natural elements like wind and rain. When it's in this tender state, you wouldn't stand there telling it to "Grow!" or asking "What's wrong with you? Why aren't you bigger and stronger yet?" Growth and resilience happen in their own time. It's the same with forgiveness.

Be gentle with yourself and trust that when it's time to forgive, it will happen naturally and spontaneously with no effort on your part. The quality of our self-care (including boundary work) and the way it improves our well-being overall can have a powerful impact on our capacity for forgiveness.

"When you are happy you can forgive a great deal."

—Princess Diana

The acting out, lies, and betrayal you've experienced as a partner of a sex addict impacted you greatly. However, I hope you will realize, either now or in the future, that what the sex addict did was completely impersonal. It had nothing to do with you, with how attractive, worthy, or lovable you are. You are all that, and more.

> When you truly understand—in your soul—that what the addict did was about him, and that you are perfect and whole just as you are, you will have moved beyond betrayal.

PARTNERS SPEAK

"I have no idea if he will slip again. He could relapse tomorrow. What I rely on today is paying attention to my reality and my intuition. That's the best I can do, day-by-day and moment by moment. With the help of my Higher Power, I know that I will be okay whether or not he continues to choose recovery."

—Lynn T.

Understanding boundaries and the way they work individually and in relationships is one of the most important self-care skills you will ever learn. Boundaries have the transformative power to create clarity and deep peace. They also make room for massive leaps in your growth and healing. When you eliminate chaos and anything in your life that holds you back from your highest good, the sky's the limit.

I'm honored to have had the opportunity to offer this information to you. My hope and wish for you is that you will take the five simple steps of the 5-SBS to create the beautiful life you deserve.

May you be firmly grounded in your own **reality**

May you know your **needs**

May you have the courage to **ask** for what you need and want

May you embrace your **authentic power** and use it wisely

May you use **boundaries** for the highest good
of yourself and others

PARTNERS SPEAK

*"I draw from the experience, strength, and hope from
a community of women on a journey. Recovery saved
my life. It allowed me to take my rightful place in life,
perfectly imperfect."*

—Paula R.

Appendix

Items marked with an asterisk (*) are adapted from the work of Pia Mellody.

5-STEP BOUNDARY SOLUTION CLARIFIER

(Available for download at www.vickitidwellpalmer.com/5sbsclarifier)

In order to identify, create, and maintain effective boundaries you must know your reality, the outcome you want, where you have power to effect change, how to take action, and how to evaluate your results. The "5-Step Boundary Solution Clarifier" is designed to guide you—step by step—through the boundary-setting process.

Step 1: Identify Your Reality

The first step is **knowing your reality**, or what is true for you about the issue you want to work on. Your reality in the present moment is what you're experiencing with your five senses (*sight, sound, smell, taste,* and *physical sensations*), what you're *thinking,* and your *emotions.* Identify your reality by asking three simple questions:

1. **Data:** What did I see/hear/experience that could be recorded with a video camera?

2. *Thought:* What is my perception/thought, or what do I "make up" about the data?

3. *Emotion:* What emotions do I feel as a result of the thought I have about the data? (Circle all that apply, and add your own as needed):

anger	pain	guilt
shame	love	fear
passion	joy	

Step 2: Identify Your Needs and Create Your Vision

Needs not currently being met with regard to this situation (circle the two to three most important needs, and add your own as needed):

affection	authenticity/genuineness
autonomy/independence	closeness/touch
communication	community
companionship	freedom
harmony	honesty
mutuality/give & take	order/reliability
peace	respect
safety	stability
support	trust

What is the outcome I want, or what is my vision, with regard to this issue? Your vision should be specific and measurable (for example: "I want my partner to call me once a day between 8:00 p.m. and 10:00 p.m. when he or she is out of town").

Step 3: Identify Your Power Center

Do you have the power to create the result you want without asking for help or making a request? If not, can you create the result you want with help from someone else, or does the result require making a request of another person? Are you powerless to create the result? Circle all that apply:

I have the power to create   I need help

I need to make a request   I am powerless

Step 4: Take Action

Based on your answer to Step 3, do one of the following:

I have the power to create the outcome:

What I need to do to create the desired outcome: _____.

I will complete this Step by (date): _____.

I need to ask for help

Seek help from _____ to create the desired outcome.

I will complete this Step by (date): _____.

I need to make a request

What is the <u>specific</u> request I need to make? Ask the person if he or she is willing to: _____ (the request must be *measurable* and *clear*). If agreed on (and applicable), this Step will be completed by (date): _____.

Do nothing

I release the problem because I'm powerless to change it, or choose to do nothing because doing nothing is the best course of action (provided I can make this choice without believing I'm a victim).

Step 5: Evaluate Your Results

If your boundary work was successful, congratulations! If the boundary missed the mark, ask:

- Did I follow through on the action I committed to in Step 4? If not, recommit or re-evaluate the action.

- If I made a request, was the agreement clear? If not, return to Step 4 and revise the request.

- Was the agreement broken (boundary violation)? If yes, determine how important this issue is to you on a scale of one to ten (ten being the greatest importance). This issue is a _____ for me. This number will help you determine your next steps.

BOUNDARY EVALUATION*

		NO BOUNDARIES/TOO VULNERABLE
EXTERNAL PHYSICAL	Protecting Self	Has trouble stopping others from getting too close physically, or accessing her private property.
	Protecting Others (Containing Self)	Often gets too close physically or touches others or their private property without permission.
EXTERNAL SEXUAL	Protecting Self	Has difficulty or does not set limits when being approached sexually.
	Protecting Others (Containing Self)	Often engages with others sexually without their agreement or permission and has trouble containing sexual energy.
INTERNAL	Listening (Protecting Self)	Often reactive to others' thoughts and emotions. Regularly takes the blame.
	Talking (Protecting Others/ Containing Self)	Often says whatever comes to mind and does not contain thoughts or emotions. Often gives the blame.

For broken agreements and boundary violations, your options are:

1. Return to Step 4 and repeat your request and/or request a repair or an amends from the other person.

2. Return to Step 4 and take necessary action, if possible, to create the result you want—or get your needs met without the participation of the other person.

3. Return to Step 1 and work Steps 1–4 based on the new issue.

4. Do nothing and accept powerlessness (provided you can let go without believing you're a victim).

WALLS/INVULNERABLE	FUNCTIONAL BOUNDARIES
Rarely lets others touch him or his private property.	Lets others know how close they can get to her physically and whether or not self or private property can be touched.
Rarely approaches others for physical touch or contact.	Respectful of others' private space and does not touch without permission.
Rarely responds to others' sexual approach, either verbally or non-verbally.	Determines who, when, where, and how she will be sexual when others approach her.
Rarely approaches others sexually or releases sexual energy.	Does not engage people sexually without their permission. Contains or releases sexual energy appropriately and in moderation.
Has difficulty listening to or taking in what is important to others.	Sorts through what others are saying and feeling; only takes in and has feelings about the truth, as he understands it.
Often does not tell others what she thinks, feels, or what is important to her.	Talks clearly in a relational and diplomatic manner. Expresses emotions with moderation.

HOW TO TAKE A RELATIONAL TIME-OUT IN SIX STEPS

1. *Recognize when you're emotionally flooded (one, or all of the following may occur)*

   - You notice *physical signs*, such as increased heart rate (over 100 bpm), changes in voice tone, heat, or skin being flushed.

   - You *shut down* and become unresponsive as a strategy to avoid conflict.

   - You *raise your voice* or begin to *communicate your anger non-verbally* by driving recklessly, slamming doors, or engaging in other threatening behavior.

2. *Communicate to your partner that you need to take a time-out*
   Tell him or her: "I'm flooded (or I'm not in a good place to have this conversation) right now, and I need to take a time-out."

3. *Tell your partner how long you need for a time-out and where you will be*
   Add additional time to your estimate to give yourself plenty of space to process what's happening for you and to get grounded and centered again.

4. *Take more time, if needed*
   If you realize while taking a time-out that you need more time, let your partner know as soon as possible.

5. *Be accountable about your commitment*
   Return at the time you stated.

6. *Re-engage about the hot-button topic*
   When you return, either ask your partner if he or she would like to re-engage about the issue or schedule a mutually agreeable time in the future to talk about it. Consider asking for a "re-do."

Time-out Dos and Don'ts:

- DO take ownership of your need for a time-out rather than rely on your partner.

- DO re-engage about the hot-button topic after a time-out.

- DON'T use time-outs as a way to avoid or delay talking about a topic that's difficult or painful for you.

- DON'T say, "You're upset and I think you need a time-out." Take ownership of your emotions and your need for a time-out.

- DON'T refuse to accept your partner's request for a time-out by physically following them, continuing to talk to them after they've requested a time-out, or refusing to let them leave.

Time-out 911:

If your partner refuses to let you leave when you ask for a time-out, you are—in essence—being held hostage. If you feel that you are in danger and that your partner has become irrational and/or dangerous, call 911.

TALKING FORMAT AND REQUEST*

When I heard you/saw you . . . (*data—what you could record with a video camera*)

What I **thought**/perceived/made up about that is . . .

And about that I feel . . . (*share your **emotions***)
Anger   pain   joy   shame   guilt   love   fear   passion

Request (*optional*)
And my request is . . .
or
Would you be willing to . . . ?

LISTENING FORMAT*

I agree/It makes sense to me that . . . (*data*)

I have the same thought/perception as you about the data.
or
I have a different thought/perception than you about the data.
Would you like to hear it? (*thought*)

I have the same thought/perception as you about the thought.
or
I have a different thought/perception than yours, would you like to hear it?

And about that, I feel . . . (*emotion*)
Anger   pain   joy   shame   guilt   love   fear   passion

NEEDS INVENTORY

Autonomy

- Choosing dreams/goals/values
- Choosing plans for fulfilling one's dreams, goals, values

Celebration

- Celebrating the creation of life and dreams fulfilled
- Celebrating losses: loved ones, dreams, etc. (mourning)

Integrity

- Authenticity
- Meaning

- Creativity
- Self-worth

Interdependence

- Appreciation
- Community
- Contribution to the enrichment of life
- Empathy
- Love
- Respect
- Trust

- Closeness
- Consideration
- Emotional Safety

- Honesty
- Reassurance
- Support
- Understanding

Physical Nurturance

- Air
- Movement, exercise
- Sexual expression
- Touch

- Food
- Rest
- Shelter
- Water

- Protection from life-threatening forms of life: viruses, bacteria, insects, predatory animals

Play

- Fun
- Spiritual Communion
- Harmony
- Order

- Laughter
- Beauty
- Inspiration
- Peace

Website: www.cnvc.org
Email: cnvc@cnvc.org
Phone: (505) 244–4041

OVERVIEW OF THE BOUNDARY SYSTEM*

Boundaries serve two primary functions:

1. Protection of self and others

2. Defining who you are by knowing and expressing your reality through your
   • Physical Body (including your appearance and physical sensations)
   • Thoughts
   • Emotions (anger, fear, pain, love, passion, shame, guilt, joy)
   • Behavior (what you do, or don't do)

There are four primary boundaries:

1. Physical Boundary
   • Protecting self: When the physical boundary of protecting yourself is functional, you let others know how close they can get to you physically and whether or not others can touch you or your private property.
   • Protecting others (containment): When the physical boundary of protecting others (sometimes referred to as containment) is functional, you are respectful of others' private space and don't touch others without permission.

2. Sexual Boundary
   • Protecting self: When the sexual boundary of protecting yourself is functional, you determine for yourself who, when, where, and how you will be sexual when others approach you.
   • Protecting others (containment): When the sexual boundary of protecting others (sometimes referred to as containment) is functional, you don't engage others

sexually without their permission and you contain or release sexual energy appropriately and in moderation.

3. Talking Boundary
   - The Talking Boundary is a boundary of protecting others (sometimes referred to as containment). When this boundary is functional, you speak clearly, in a relational and diplomatic manner. You express emotions with moderation.

4. Listening Boundary
   - The Listening Boundary is primarily a boundary of protecting the self. When this boundary is functional, you listen with curiosity and sort through the thoughts

---

STAGES OF HEALING FOR PARTNERS OF SEX ADDICTS

(Adapted from *Mending a Shattered Heart: A Guide for Partners of Sex Addicts* by Stefanie Carnes et al., 2008)

STAGE	CHARACTERISTICS
Developing/ Pre-Discovery Partners begin to understand that their loved one has a problem and that something has to be done	• having hunch something isn't right • self-doubt, second guessing, not trusting gut feelings • tolerating and normalizing unacceptable behavior from the addict, such as lying, verbal abuse, dependency, unavailability, mood swings • compromising values, morals, or beliefs for the sake of keeping the peace
Crisis/Decision Partners realize they can no longer tolerate the problem	• discovery and/or disclosure • information gathering (seeking a false sense of safety through checking behaviors and preoccupation with addict's behavior)

and emotions being expressed by the other person. You only take in as truth (as you understand it) the thoughts that match your perceptions, and any emotions that arise as a result of your thoughts about what you've heard.

There is also a fifth boundary—the "personal energy boundary." Personal energy is not necessarily something you can hear or see, but is rather an intuitive or "felt sense" of a person that extends or radiates beyond the physical body. The personal energy boundary is primarily a protective boundary, meaning that when you sense the energy of another person and inadvertently "pick up" their emotions or other negative internal states, you can intentionally activate or create an internal boundary of protection. (See Chapter Three for more information about the personal energy boundary.)

ROADBLOCKS TO NAVIGATING STAGE	TIPS FOR SUCCESSFUL NAVIGATION
• low intimacy expectations due to disengaged relational style of family of origin • awareness of own reality is significantly damaged • addict is highly skilled in maintaining deception or behavior has low probability of discovery	• focus on own reality (thoughts, emotions, action) • trust intuition • know and honor your values, morals, and beliefs
• believing "if he stops acting out all my problems will be solved" • believing "if I were only _____ he would stop acting out" • obsession/rumination • ignoring own reality and believing addict's lies	• focus information gathering on problem vs. addict • practice regular self-care • trust intuition • continued focus on own reality • celibacy

STAGE	CHARACTERISTICS
Shock Partners absorb the reality of how bad things have gotten and seek help	• emotional numbness or avoidance • feelings of victimization • suspiciousness/distrust • terror about slips, relapse • relational conflict • feelings of despair • anger, hostility, self-righteousness, blame, and criticism
Grief Partners understand their losses and pain—specifically how the addict's behavior fits the larger patterns of his or her life	• depression • ambivalence about relationship • increased introspection and focus on self
Repair Partners reconstruct how they interact with themselves and those around them	• introspection • decision-making stage about relationship • deeper insight into causes of own issues • prior losses more fully grieved • increased strength and coping skills • greater emotional stability
Growth Partners experience a new depth in their relationships and a new level of openness and effectiveness	• decreased feelings of being victimized by addiction • focus on issues not directly related to addiction • communication skills and conflict resolution styles explored • awareness and accountability of role in relational dysfunction • acknowledgment of gifts the addiction has brought to your life • ability to be present and more fully focused on other areas of life

ROADBLOCKS TO NAVIGATING STAGE	TIPS FOR SUCCESSFUL NAVIGATION
• retreating into denial to avoid painful feelings and difficult work • making major decisions prematurely • "unbridled self-expression" (offending from the victim position)	• seek information and specialized help • begin to utilize all available resources (individual/group therapy, twelve-step, workshops/retreats, reading material) • focus on self-care • identify areas of vulnerability (emotional support, financial, physical, etc.)
• depression/anxiety not addressed • failure to get help for trauma • rush to forgiveness • taking role of authority figure with addict • establishing unreasonable non-negotiables • getting stuck in victim role and focusing on addict's behavior	• identify and grieve losses • trauma work with therapist and group (incident writing, "worst moments") • learning to accept "not knowing" • assess with therapist need for medication evaluation • begin to identify own issues (current and family of origin)
• imbalance between individual and couples' work • failure to acknowledge addict's recovery behaviors (stuck in past) • failure to address family of origin issues/trauma • mistaking trauma bonding (intensity) for intimacy	• boundary work • increase focus on couples' work (therapy, workshops, Recovering Couples Anonymous)
• failure to address couples' issues (e.g., finances, parenting, in-law relationships) • failure to address couples' sexual reintegration	• intensive couples' work (boundaries, communication, sexual reintegration) • increase focus on own interests apart from relationship (e.g., hobbies, friends, vocation) • strengthen support system outside primary relationship

SUGGESTED RECOVERY CHECK-IN ITEMS FOR SEX ADDICTS AND THEIR PARTNERS

Except for sobriety date, addict and partner may *both* check in regarding the following:

1. Sobriety date from inner circle behaviors (this should be the first item on any couples' recovery check-in)

2. Feelings: How I'm feeling now (anger, pain, guilt, love, joy, shame, fear, passion)

3. Recovery activities since last check-in (twelve-step meetings, group therapy, individual and/or couples' therapy, reading, homework, step work)

4. Optional: Triggers addict experienced and tools used to deal with triggers. For example, "This week I was triggered several times and when that happened, I said the serenity prayer/called a program person or sponsor/redirected my attention [or whatever tool was used]."

   Emphasis is on tools used rather than details of triggers. For example, if addict was triggered by a particular person, the focus is on the tools used to deal with the trigger rather than what the person looked like, what they were wearing, etc. Addict may rate the intensity of the trigger on a scale of one to ten, ten being the highest.

Couples Check-in (optional):

• What you (your partner) did that helped the relationship.

• What I did that harmed the relationship.

• Express an appreciation for the other person. For example, "I appreciate the way you took care of our daughter this week when she was sick."

Check-in Dos and Don'ts

- Addict should take responsibility to initiate check-ins.

- DO make sobriety date the first item on any recovery check-in. Partners are often anxious waiting to hear this information and may miss other details as they are waiting to hear the sobriety date.

- DO schedule regular check-ins with a specific start and end time. For example, every Sunday night from 6:00 p.m. to 6:20 p.m. or every Tuesday morning from 7:00 a.m. to 7:20 a.m.

- DON'T share middle circle behaviors (specifically objectification, euphoric recall, fantasy, etc.) unless they have significantly impacted the addict's recovery that week or have interfered with the couple's communication or connection.

- DO (for the addict) make an effort to minimize defensiveness if your partner asks questions about your check-in or needs more information.

- DO (for the partner) listen to the check-in without interrupting and thank the addict when complete.

- DO (for the partner) mindfully consider the questions you want to ask the addict regarding his or her triggers and middle circle behavior. This information (especially if it relates only to thoughts and/or fantasies) is generally more harmful than helpful to the partner and the couple.

FINDING YOUR ADVERSE CHILDHOOD EXPERIENCES (ACE) SCORE

(ACEstudy.org)

While you were growing up, during your first eighteen years of life:

1. Did a parent or other adult in the household **often or very often** swear at you, insult you, put you down, or humiliate you?

    or

    Act in a way that made you afraid that you might be physically hurt?

    ○ Yes   ○ No   If yes enter 1 _____

2. Did a parent or other adult in the household **often or very often** push, grab, slap, or throw something at you?

    or

    Ever hit you so hard that you had marks or were injured?

    ○ Yes   ○ No   If yes enter 1 _____

3. Did an adult or person at least five years older than you **ever** touch or fondle you or have you touch his or her body in a sexual way?

    or

    Attempt or actually have oral, anal, or vaginal intercourse with you?

    ○ Yes   ○ No   If yes enter 1 _____

4. Did you **often or very often** feel that no one in your family loved you or thought you were important or special?

    or

Your family didn't look out for each other, feel close to each other, or support each other?

○ Yes   ○ No   **If yes enter 1** _____

5. Did you **often or very often** feel that you didn't have enough to eat, had to wear dirty clothes, and had no one to protect you?

> **or**

Your parents were too drunk or high to take care of you or take you to the doctor if you needed it?

○ Yes   ○ No   **If yes enter 1** _____

6. Were your parents **ever** separated or divorced?

○ Yes   ○ No   **If yes enter 1** _____

7. Was your mother or stepmother **often or very often** pushed, grabbed, slapped, or had something thrown at her?

> **or**

Sometimes, often, or very often kicked, bitten, hit with a fist, or hit with something hard?

> **or**

Ever repeatedly hit at least a few minutes or threatened with a gun or knife?

○ Yes   ○ No   **If yes enter 1** _____

8. Did you live with anyone who was a problem drinker or alcoholic or who used street drugs?

○ Yes   ○ No   **If yes enter 1** _____

9. Was a household member depressed or mentally ill, or did a household member attempt suicide?

○ Yes   ○ No   If yes enter 1 _____

10. Did a household member go to prison?

○ Yes   ○ No   If yes enter 1 _____

Now add up your "Yes" answers: _____
This is your ACE Score

Individuals scoring three or higher were at significantly higher risk for chronic disease, drug use, suicide, engaging in violence, or being a victim of violence.[10]

---

[10] Jane Ellen Stevens, "Spokane, WA Students' Trauma Prompts Search for Solutions," blog post on *ACEsTooHigh*, 28 February, 2012, acestoohigh.com/2012/02/28/spokane-wa-students-child-trauma-prompts-search-for-prevention.

LOVE ADDICTION TEST

The following questions are a guide to help you determine whether or not love addiction may be an issue for you. Love addiction is not a mental health diagnosis; however, it is a real and debilitating condition. If you answer "yes" to more than five questions, further assessment by a mental health treatment provider is recommended.

1. Have you made excuses for the sex addict's behavior or told yourself that his/her addiction is your fault?

2. Have you ever tried to control how much sex to have or how often you would see someone?

3. Do you find yourself unable to stop seeing a specific person even though you know that seeing this person is destructive to you?

4. Do you get "high" from sex and/or romance? Do you crash?

5. Have you ever believed that if a romantic relationship ended you wouldn't be able to live without the other person?

6. Do you make promises to yourself or rules for yourself concerning your sexual or romantic behavior that you find you cannot follow?

7. Have you had or do you have sex with the addict when you didn't want to?

8. Do you believe that sex and/or being in a relationship will make your life bearable?

9. When you were growing up, did you often feel invisible or that your parents (or caregivers) didn't truly know or "see" you?

10. Do you believe that someone can "fix" you?

11. Do you feel desperation or uneasiness when you are away from your lover or sexual partner?

12. Do you feel desperate about your need for a partner or future mate?

13. Do you find that you have a pattern of repeating bad relationships?

14. Do you feel that you're not "really alive" unless you are with your sexual/romantic partner?

15. Do you find yourself in a relationship that you cannot leave?

16. Do you feel that life would have no meaning without a love relationship or without sex?

17. Do you feel that you would have no identity if you were not someone's lover?

18. Do you find yourself flirting or sexualizing with someone even if you do not mean to?

19. Do you need to have sex, or "fall in love" in order to feel like a "real man" or a "real woman"?

20. Are you unable to concentrate on other areas of your life because of thoughts or feelings you are having about another person or about sex?

21. Do you find yourself obsessing about a specific person or sexual act even though these thoughts bring pain, craving, or discomfort?

22. Have you ever wished you could stop or control your sexual and romantic activities for a given period of time? Have you ever wished you could be less emotionally dependent?

23. Are you afraid that deep down you are unacceptable?

24. Do you feel that your life is unmanageable because of your sexual and/or romantic behavior or your excessive dependency needs?

25. Have you ever thought there might be more you could do with your life if you were not so driven by sexual and romantic pursuits?

Adapted from "40 Questions for Self Diagnosis" by The Augustine Fellowship, S.L.A.A., Fellowship-Wide Services, Inc. and Pia Mellody's "Love Addiction Memory Jogger."

Recommended Reading

PARTNERS OF SEX ADDICTS

Black, C. *Deceived.* Center City, MN: Hazelden, 2009.

Black, C., and Tripodi, C. *Intimate Treason: Healing the Trauma for Partners Confronting Sex Addiction.* Las Vegas, NV: Central Recovery Press, 2012.

Carnes, S. *Mending a Shattered Heart: A Guide for Partners of Sex Addicts.* Carefree, AZ: Gentle Path Press, 2011.

Carnes, S., Lee, M., and Rodriguez, A. *Facing Heartbreak: Steps to Recovery for Partners of Sex Addicts.* Carefree, AZ: Gentle Path Press, 2012.

Kort, J. *Is My Husband Gay, Straight, or Bi? A Guide for Women Concerned about Their Men.* Lanham, MD: Rowman & Littlefield, 2014.

Schneider, J. *Back From Betrayal: Recovering from the Trauma of Infidelity.* North Charleston, SC: CreateSpace, 2015.

Schneider, J., and Corley, M. *Surviving Disclosure: A Partner's Guide for Healing the Betrayal of Intimate Trust.* North Charleston, SC: CreateSpace, 2012.

Schneider, J., and Corley, M. *Disclosing Secrets: An Addict's Guide for When, to Whom, and How Much to Reveal.* North Charleston, SC: CreateSpace, 2012.

Steffens, B., and Means, M. *Your Sexually Addicted Spouse: How Partners Can Cope and Heal.* Far Hills, NJ: New Horizon Press, 2009.

SEX ADDICTION

Canning, M. *Lust, Anger, Love: Understanding Sexual Addiction and the Road to Healthy Intimacy.* Naperville, IL: Sourcebooks, Inc., 2008.

Carnes, P. *Out of the Shadows: Understanding Sexual Addiction.* Center City, MN: Hazelden, 2001.

Carnes, P. *Sexual Anorexia: Overcoming Sexual Self-Hatred.* Center City, MN: Hazelden, 1997.

Magness, M. *Stop Sex Addiction: Real Hope, True Freedom for Sex Addicts and Partners.* Las Vegas, NV: Central Recovery Press, 2013.

Maltz, W., and Maltz, L. *The Porn Trap: The Essential Guide to Overcoming Problems Caused by Pornography.* New York: HarperCollins Publishers, 2008.

Weiss, R. *Cruise Control: Understanding Sex Addiction in Gay Men.* Carefree, AZ: Gentle Path Press, 2013.

COUPLES/COMMUNICATION

Bercaw, B., and Bercaw, G. *The Couple's Guide to Intimacy: How Sexual Reintegration Therapy Can Help Your Relationship Heal.* Pasadena, CA: CreateSpace, 2010.

Glass, S. *Not "Just Friends": Rebuilding Trust and Recovering Your Sanity After Infidelity.* New York: Free Press, 2004.

Katehakis, A., and Bliss, T. *Mirror of Intimacy: Daily Reflections on Emotional and Erotic Intelligence*. Los Angeles, CA: Center for Healthy Sex, 2014.

Mellody, P. *The Intimacy Factor: The Ground Rules for Overcoming the Obstacles to Truth, Respect, and Lasting Love*. New York: HarperOne Publishers, 2004.

Rosenberg, M. *Nonviolent Communication: A Language of Life*. Encinitas, CA: PuddleDancer Press, 2003.

SEX AND LOVE ADDICTION

McDaniel, K. *Ready to Heal: Breaking Free of Addictive Relationships*. Carefree, AZ: Gentle Path Press, 2012.

Mellody, P., Miller, A., and Miller, J. *Facing Love Addiction: Giving Yourself the Power to Change the Way You Love*. New York: HarperOne Publishers, 2003.

FAMILY OF ORIGIN AND TRAUMA

Bradshaw, J. *Healing the Shame that Binds You*. Deerfield Beach, FL: Health Communications, Inc., 2005.

Carnes, P. *The Betrayal Bond: Breaking Free of Exploitive Relationships*. Deerfield Beach, FL: Health Communications, Inc., 1997.

Levine, P. *Waking the Tiger: Healing Trauma*. Berkeley, CA: North Atlantic Books, 1997.

Mellody, P., and Miller, A. *Breaking Free. A Recovery Workbook for Facing Codependence*. New York: HarperCollins Publishers, 1989.

Mellody, P. and Miller, A., and Miller, J. *Facing Codependence: What It Is, Where It Comes from, How It Sabotages Our Lives*. New York: HarperCollins Publishers, 2003.

Resources for Partners of Sex Addicts

TRAUMA RESOURCES

Eye Movement Desensitization and Reprocessing (EMDR)
www.emdria.org
(866) 451–5200

Healing Trauma Network
Network of therapists trained in Pia Mellody's Post Induction
Therapy Model
www.healingtraumanetwork.net
(781) 777–1172

Sensorimotor Psychotherapy Institute
www.sensorimotorpsychotherapy.org
(800) 860–9258

Somatic Experiencing® Trauma Institute
Find a certified Somatic Experiencing® Practitioner (SEP)
www.traumahealing.org
(303) 652–4035

INTENSIVES AND IN-PATIENT TREATMENT CENTERS SPECIALIZING IN PARTNER-SPECIFIC TREATMENT

Bethesda Workshops (Christian-based)
www.bethesdaworkshops.org
3710 Franklin Pike
Nashville, TN 37204
(615) 467–5610

Center for Healthy Sex
www.centerforhealthysex.com
10700 Santa Monica Boulevard, Suite 311
Los Angeles, CA 90025
(310) 843–9902

Kenneth M. Adams & Associates
www.sexualhealth-addiction.com
26862 Woodward Avenue, Suite 102
Royal Oak, MI 48067
(248) 398–0740 ext. 1

The Meadows
Offers a workshop titled "Healing Intimate Treason: For Partners of Sex Addicts"
www.themeadows.com
1655 N. Tegner Street
Wickenburg, AZ 85390
(800) 632–3697

Onsite
www.onsiteworkshops.com
1044 Old Highway 48
Cumberland Furnace, TN 37051
(800) 341–7432

The Refuge
Treatment center specializing in trauma and PTSD
www.therefuge-ahealingplace.com
14835 SE 85th
Ocklawaha, FL 32179
(866) 473–3843

ONLINE RESOURCES
The Center for Nonviolent Communication
www.cnvc.org
(800) 255–7696

Dear Peggy
Extramarital Affairs Resource Center
www.dearpeggy.com

International Institute for Trauma & Addiction Professionals (IITAP)
Screening instruments and information about sex addiction, partner sexuality, trauma, and betrayal bonding
www.sexhelp.com
(866) 575–6853

National Domestic Violence Hotline
www.ndvh.org
(800) 799–7233
(800) 737–3224 TTY for the Deaf

MISCELLANEOUS RESOURCES
American Board of Psychiatry and Neurology, Inc.
Find a board certified psychiatrist
www.abpn.com
(847) 229–6500

Association of Partners of Sex Addicts Trauma Specialists
Find a Certified Clinical Partner Specialist (CCPS) or Certified
Partner Coach (CPC)
www.apsats.org
(513) 644–8023

Dialectical Behavior Therapy (DBT)
Treatment for a wide range of disorders including emotional
regulation, substance dependence, depression, PTSD, and eating
disorders
www.behavioraltech.org
(206) 675–8588

Society for the Advancement of Sexual Health (SASH)
Find therapists with experience treating partners of sex addicts and
sex addicts.
www.sash.net
(610) 348–4783

The following online assessments developed by the International
Institute of Trauma & Addiction Professionals (IITAP), are available
through Certified Sex Addiction Therapists (CSATs) for partners of
sex addicts:

Partner Sexuality Survey (PSS)
The PSS was designed by Dr. Stefanie Carnes to assist partners in
identifying areas of his or her own sexuality that may have been
impacted by his or her relationship with the sex addict.

Inventory for Partner Anxiety, Stress, and Trauma (IPAST)
The IPAST is a battery of assessments that examine partners'
traumatic reactions, family of origin, strengths, and attachment styles.

Post-Traumatic Stress Inventory (PTSI)

The PTSI was designed to assess current style of functioning, related to past or current trauma.

SEX ADDICTION INTENSIVES AND IN-PATIENT TREATMENT

Bellwood Health Services

www.bellwood.ca
1020 McNicoll Avenue
Toronto, ON, Canada M1W 2J6
(800) 387–6198

Center for Healthy Sex

www.centerforhealthysex.com
10700 Santa Monica Boulevard, Suite 311
Los Angeles, CA 90025
(310) 843–9902

Elements Behavioral Health

www.elementsbehavioralhealth.com
5000 E. Spring Street, Suite 650
Long Beach, CA 90815
(844) 857–4766

Hope & Freedom Counseling Services

www.hopeandfreedom.com
3730 Kirby Drive, Suite 1130
Houston, TX 77098
(713) 630–0111

Keystone Center Extended Care Unit

www.keystonecenterecu.net
2000 Providence Avenue
Chester, PA 19013
(800) 733–6840

Life Healing Center

www.life-healing.com
25 Vista Point Road
Santa Fe, NM 87508
(866) 806–7214

The Meadows – Gentle Path

www.themeadows.com
1655 N. Tegner Street
Wickenburg, AZ 85390
(800) 244–4949

Pine Grove – Gratitude Program

www.pinegrovetreatment.com
2255 Broadway Drive
Hattiesburg, MS 39402
(888) 574–4673

Psychological Counseling Services

www.pcsearle.com
7530 E. Angus Drive
Scottsdale, AZ 85251
(480) 947–5739

Santé Center for Healing

www.santecenter.com
914 Country Club Road
Argyle, TX 76226
(800) 258–4250

Vicki Tidwell Palmer Resources and Programs

Complete 5-Step Boundary Solution Clarifier (PDF Version).
Free instant access downloadable PDF at: www.vickitidwellpalmer.
com/5sbsclarifier.

5-Step Boundary Solution Quick-Start Guide:
The 5-SBS Quick-Start Guide outlines the fundamental concepts
behind the 5-SBS method of boundary setting. Instructions for each
step are included, along with the 5-Step Boundary Solution Clarifier.
Downloadable PDF available online at: www.vickitidwellpalmer.
com/5sbsquickstartguide.

***Moving Beyond Betrayal* Online Course:**
This online course is for serious students of the 5-SBS who want to go
even deeper into developing their boundary skills. The course includes
live Q&A sessions where participants have the opportunity to get their
questions answered directly from Vicki. To register online go to www.
vickitidwellpalmer.com.

5-Step Boundary Solution Intensives for Partners of Sex Addicts:

The 5-SBS Intensive is a rare opportunity to work with Vicki in person in a small, intimate community with other partners of sex addicts. Intensives are held at Vicki's office in Houston, Texas, and are limited to eight participants. For more information go to www.vickitidwellpalmer.com.

5-Step Boundary Solution Boundaries Coaching Intensive for Partners of Sex Addicts and Survivors of Infidelity:

The 5-SBS Intensives are virtual, one-on-one deep dives into boundary work personally facilitated by Vicki. Intensives are by application only and are tailored to the partner's goals and needs. For more information or to apply for a 5-SBS Intensive, go to www.vickitidwellpalmer.com.

Taming Triggers Solution (TTS) Online Course: 7 Steps for Creating Calm in the Storm for Partners of Sex Addicts and Survivors of Infidelity:

The TTS Online Course outlines a seven-step system to help partners of sex addicts and survivors of infidelity learn skills and tools for reducing or eliminating the many distressing triggers that are part of the discovery and disclosure process.

Partners of Sex Addicts Blog:

Visit Vicki's blog, *Survival Strategies for Partners of Sex Addicts*, at www.vickitidwellpalmer.com.

Family of Origin Intensives:

Vicki offers four-day family of origin trauma intensives, *Reclaiming Wholeness*, through her private practice. For more information or to register, go to www.vickitidwellpalmer.com/workshops.

Also Available from Central Recovery Press

SEX ADDICTION
Behavioral Addiction: Screening, Assessment, and Treatment
An-Pyng Sun, PhD; Larry Ashley, EdS; Lesley Dickson, MD • $18.95
US • ISBN: 978-1-936290-97-0 • E-book: 978-1-937612-05-4

Stop Sex Addiction: Real Hope, True Freedom for Sex Addicts and Partners
Milton S. Magness, D.Min. • $17.95 US • ISBN: 978-1-937612-23-8 •
E-book: 978-1-937612-24-5

Intimate Treason: Healing the Trauma for Partners Confronting Sex Addiction
Claudia Black, PhD and Cara Tripodi, LCSW • $17.95 US • ISBN:
978-1-936290-93-2 • E-book: 978-1-937612-01-6

RELATIONSHIPS AND EMOTIONAL HEALTH
Irrelationship: How We Use Dysfunctional Relationships to Hide from Intimacy
Mark Borg, Jr., PhD; Grant Brenner, MD; Daniel Berry, RN, MHA •
$16.95 US • ISBN: 978-1-942094-00-5 • E-book: 978-1-942094-01-2

A Spiritual Path to a Healthy Relationship: A Practical Approach
Steve McCord, MFT and Angie McCord, CC • $15.95 US • ISBN: 978-1-936290-65-9 • E-book: 978-1-936290-77-2

Disentangle: When You've Lost Your Self in Someone Else
Nancy L. Johnston, MS, LPC, LSATP • $15.95 US • ISBN: 978-1-936290-03-1 • E-book: 978-1-936290-49-9

Dancing in the Dark: How to Take Care of Yourself When Someone You Love Is Depressed
Bernadette Stankard and Amy Viets • $15.95 US • ISBN: 978-1-936290-70-3 • E-book: 978-1-936290-83-3

A Man's Way through Relationships: Learning to Love and Be Loved
Dan Griffin, MA • $15.95 US • ISBN: 978-1-937612-66-5 • E-book: 978-1-937612-67-2

Game Plan: A Man's Guide to Achieving Emotional Fitness
Alan P. Lyme; David J. Powell, PhD; Stephen R Andrew, LCSW • $15.95 US • ISBN: 978-1-936290-96-3 • E-book: 978-1-937612-04-7

Hard to Love: Understanding and Overcoming Male Borderline Personality Disorder
Joseph Nowinski, PhD • $15.95 US • ISBN: 978-1-937612-57-3 • E-book: 978-1-937612-58-0

Dark Wine Waters: My Husband of a Thousand Joys and Sorrows
Fran Simone, PhD • $15.95 US • ISBN: 978-1-937612-64-1 • E-book: 978-1-937612-65-8